You are Light

8 Words Reveal Your Truest Self

You are Light

8 Words Reveal Your Truest Self

Monica McDowell, MDiv

BOOKS

Winchester, UK
Washington, USA

First published by O-Books, 2010
O Books is an imprint of John Hunt Publishing Ltd., The Bothy, Deershot Lodge, Park Lane, Ropley,
Hants, SO24 0BE, UK
office1@o-books.net
www.o-books.com

For distributor details and how to order please visit the 'Ordering' section on our website.

Text copyright Monica McDowell 2010

ISBN: 978 1 84694 436 9

Design: Stuart Davies

Printed in the UK by CPI Antony Rowe
Printed in the USA by Offset Paperback Mfrs, Inc

We operate a distinctive and ethical publishing philosophy in all
areas of its business, from its global network of authors to
production and worldwide distribution.

CONTENTS

Also by Monica McDowell

My Karma Ran Over My Dogma:
Lessons Learned by a Whistle-Blowing Minister Turned Mystic

Dedicated to my beloved children,
Landon and Lindsay,
two lights who shine bright in my life

Introduction

A new day dawns,
The sun rises in your heart,
You awaken to your Truest Self.

Suddenly, the entire world becomes your home: the animals your companions, the planets and stars your guides, the trees your protectors. Everyone emerges as a perfect reflection of your own precious soul. Eight words reveal the full complement of your Truest Self. The first word is **Light**, followed by seven equally significant words. Just as white light is refracted into the seven spectral colors of the rainbow, so too, these seven words flesh out what it means to be Light in living form.

Awakening is both a point in time and a journey through time. It is a marvelous beginning and also a process of working out the full implications of what awakening means. Once you have awakened to your Truest Self, nothing can be the same again and yet, you still live out the life that is in front of you.

This meditation book will help you to awaken, as well as learn how to apply your new awareness to everyday life. Each chapter focuses on one of the eight illuminated words and ends with a workbook section to help you connect directly with this quality of your Truest Self. It is important to note that meditation is not an end it itself. Meditation is a means, a tool, to help you create the space wherein your Truest Self can be discovered and remembered, and then to help you fully embody and consciously live your life from this sacred place.

There are two ways I suggest utilizing this book. One way is to read it through slowly in a contemplative fashion, gradually completing the workbooks as you go. Another way, especially good for those of you new to meditation, is to read through the book in its entirety without doing the workbooks. Then, re-read the chapter that has the most appeal for you, completing the associated workbook at that time.

You may want to focus on a particular chapter for a week, a month, or longer. It is not necessary or even desirable to do all the chapters and workbooks within a short period of time. Because everything is interconnected, by focusing on one area, you are in the end, helping to heal and awaken all of you. Transformation, whether for a person, butterfly, or even an apple tree, requires the full cycle of seasons to come to fruition, so work through the book gently and reflectively. There is no rush. You have all the time you need.

I compiled the words for this book, because the dawning of one's Truest Self requires a new scripture, if you will—something to draw the soul upward and forward as it integrates Light into the here and now. Ultimately, though, "God" is beyond all names, all words, and all language. In fact, language itself is a filter, a perceptual lens through which we see the world. At any given moment, we can perceive and process only a fraction of the infinite amounts of sensory data right in front of our eyes. Human concepts are simply inadequate to express or explain *All That Is*. For how can sunlight be captured?

Thus, in my compilation of these eight words, I have not written: "This is what God said." Rather, I have stated: "I heard the Divine say..." My words are derivative at best. Decide for yourself whether they ring true for your heart and soul. If there are some concepts that do not resonate with you, please disregard them. My hope, though, is that you will be richly blessed with the fullness of life in the reading and practicing of these words.

—**Monica McDowell**
Seattle, Washington
December 2009

You are Light

I heard the Divine say, "Tell the people:

"You are Light. The Divine Spark within you shines brighter than ten thousand suns. You are an eternally burning ember in the flame of God.

"You are this Light. This is who you *really* are. You are always in this Light and this Light is always in you.

"This Light that is in you, that is you, is the Light that shines in all. If you look closely into another's eyes, you might just see this One Light shining. It is always there. Never despair.

"The Light that is in me is the Light that is in you. There is no separation, no division, only distinction. At your core, we are One.

"I am Infinite Light; you cannot reach the end. You, too, are this Light at your core, at your Truest Self. What does this mean for your life? So many things!

"'You are Light' may sound ethereal but even your science says that material forms are simply dense energy or slowed-down light. The old scientific models of the universe are breaking down and new models are emerging that show the interconnection of all and that all is one. Science reveals that all matter is a form of energy or light or vibration. This is true not only of your body, but your consciousness is also a form of energy.

"The various manifested forms of Light are temporary, even the earth, the sun, and stars all have a designated time of life, just as your body and all bodies do. But your consciousness is eternally alive in Spirit. Your consciousness and the energy of all are held within a portion of the divine mind. You are always held.

"You are always Light. The Truest You is always Light. Your awareness, your consciousness, and your body are at varying degrees of Light.

"The more your consciousness expands, the more your Light expands. It is important to integrate this Light into your entire being, bringing more Light to each area.

"Your awareness or your consciousness is in various stages of development. Sometimes you turn away from this Light and your shadow grows. But the Light is still there, ever-beckoning and ever-strong, just dimmed by the heaviness of your thoughts, emotions, actions, and beliefs that do not reflect your Truest Nature.

"Then, at the right time, you turn towards Light again, cleaning, clearing, purifying your thoughts, actions, emotions and beliefs so that the Light shines through you more clearly and more radiantly.

"Your Light is always radiant, yet you do not always show that radiance. It is important to integrate your shadow and clear away the heavy non-beneficial debris that has accumulated on the jewel of your Light.

"You are always growing, always expanding. If you practice these things, your whole body will be brighter than the noonday sun.

"The Light is always there, ever-beckoning, ever-growing, ever-steady, and ever-radiant. Be Light. Be the Light that you are.

"You are never truly cut off from the Light. You are always Light. Always. Can you find that pure ray in yourself? You can. Find it and you will know you are home and always have been.

"Light from the all-dwelling, ever-present Life is always in you. Always with you. Always aware of every facet of your being. This Light gives life to all. This Light is the Truest You.

"When you live in this Light, you dwell in the Love that birthed the worlds. You live in the Light of the universes. You dwell in the Presence. Then you know you are never alone and that you are always connected and always part of the One, the Beloved, the Source.

"This Light can heal anything. This Light is the way back home. This Light is the realization that at your core you never left home. You are always home.

"Vast numbers of beings forever dwell in this Light, ever-loving, ever-caring, ever-leading, and ever-healing. The array of these beings is so bright that your sun looks dim in comparison. They are ever-present, ever with you, ever-guarding, and ever-guiding.

"They reflect the numinosity as well as the luminosity of the Great Spirit. They reflect the Love found in the Divine Heart. Ever so gently they speak. In deep silence you can hear them. They are the voices of Love and Light. There is no judgment here—only Love. It is a Love so rich that all the world's ills are but a small wrinkle on the face of eternity.

"You are always Light. This Light is ever with you. You can always connect with this Light wherever you are, whatever you are doing.

"Envision this Light; it comes down from above through the top of your head, filling your body with pure golden, loving, healing light. Can you feel this? Do not worry if you can only imagine that you see it and feel it. This is enough. Soon you *will* see it and feel it. You are loved more deeply than words can express.

"Light, inaccessible Light, more radiant and glorious to behold than ten thousand suns—this mystery beyond all is life. This mystery is holding you in tender embracing love, always and forever. You are a creation of the Divine Mind.

"Blessed be the One who is ever and always in inaccessible glory and majesty. Your Truest Self is there: ever-present, ever-aware, ever-becoming and growing, and ever-alive. No thought can contain the great Beingness. No human mind can comprehend the infinite vastness of the mystery that births the multitudinous forms of manifested light.

"Beyond all, yet in all, this Light comprehends the minds of everyone. This Light is in you like a ray of sun that grows ever-brighter with your ever-growing and expanding awareness.

"There is no need to worry at all. This Light holds you dearer than you can imagine. You are blessed. You are beloved. You are an ever-shining Light.

"Be not afraid. There is no reason to be so. Never be afraid, for your future is Light and in the dissolution of time, your past, present, and future are all Light. The Light may be hidden from your eyes for a moment, like the sun temporarily hidden behind the passing cloud, but it is always present and always there.

"There is nothing and no one to fear. Everything is manifested from the Divine Mind. Truly no harm may come to you. You are ever-present and ever-growing. You have come so far and you have infinite reaches to expand to. Seek this Light and Love.

"You are growing into the Light at the right pace for you. Light is ever-growing, ever-blessing, and ever-full."

I heard the Divine say,
"All is well.
"All is well.
"All is well.

"Blessings of the Light be with you and your loved ones now and forevermore."

WORKBOOK

The workbooks at the end of each chapter are designed to help you find your own intuitive guidance. They include questions, affirmations, and meditations with space to journal and write your own reflections. These exercises will help you seek the Light within and wait for the answers that will be given to you. The workbooks may also be used for group practice and discussion.

If you are new to meditation, here are some suggestions to help you. First, find a peaceful place in your home, office building, or somewhere in nature where you will not be interrupted. Once you are settled, take some time to breathe slowly into your belly focusing only on the breath. When you are calm, center your attention deep within your being and say to yourself or out loud, "I open myself to receive with gratitude whatever is for my highest and best in joy at this time." Then, as you contemplate the following questions and practice the meditations and affirmations, try to stay centered deep within and see what answers and insights come to you from that place. It can take some practice to shift from your rational, left-brain oriented way of thinking to a body and whole-being centered awareness, so be kind and gentle with yourself as you learn, grow, and awaken.

Questions

- What does "You are Light" mean to you?

- When have you felt a connection to *All That Is* or had an experience with Light? Describe the experience with as many sensory details as you can recall (sights, sounds, smells, feelings, etc.) What impact did it have on your life?

- How is this concept—that your Truest Self is Light—similar to or different than what you were raised to believe? What emotions arise in you about this?

- What does this Light mean for someone living through a dark night of the soul?

- What questions does the phrase "your Truest Self is a divine spark" raise for you in your life? What answers does it provide?

- Write, say, sing, or paint the word "Light" up to 100 times slowly. What thoughts, feelings, resistances, and physical sensations come into your awareness as you do this?

- How can you move toward becoming more of the Light that you are? How do you best reflect this Light in your life already?

Meditations

The following spiritual practices are designed to help you incorporate this new understanding of who you are into your daily life.

Core Star Meditation

The Divine Spark in you is sometimes called the Core Star. Seers, mystics, and healers probably call it this because that is exactly what it looks like: a radiant star centered in your being with rays of brilliant, white light bursting forth in all directions. For this meditation, focus your attention within at what feels like the deepest, most centered place in your body. Imagine you can see this core star within you. What do you see? What do you feel? Imagine that this core star is growing larger and larger until your entire body is within it. Carry this image with you throughout your day and imprint it in your mind right before you go to sleep. This will bring you healing and protection and help you feel vibrant and strong!

Write down any new questions, insights, or experiences here.

Oneness Meditation

You are one with all, so practice this today. Whomever you run into, remind yourself that they, too, at their core are one with the Divine Light of all. No matter how they look or how they are acting, pretend that you can see through the disguise, the mirage, and see Light in that person's eyes. Regard each person as if they are an embodiment of this Light. Treat them with love, respect, kindness, generosity, gratitude, and honor. In the Christian mystical tradition, this is the practice of "seeing the Christ in all." In the Hindu tradition, this is practiced by bowing and saying, "Namaste" which means, "the Divine in me recognizes the Divine in you."

Of course, this is the most powerful with people difficult to befriend. There is a Tibetan saying, "The enemy is our greatest teacher because only the enemy can teach us patience and compassion." So, be aware, the universe may test you here and there. You might get a cantankerous customer on the phone, or your grumpy neighbor might say something very unkind. That is okay. See through the surface reality to the deeper underlying reality: They, too, are Light. If you stay in your awareness of this while you interact with people, you might find some very surprising changes in their behavior!

Increase your time doing this practice until you can sustain it as long as you want and until it becomes a reality in your everyday awareness.

Reflect on how this effects your interactions with your family, co-workers, friends, and with strangers. Are there any significant differences in your relationships? Have you noticed any changes in your thoughts, emotions, and actions?

Write down any new questions, insights, or experiences here.

Affirmations

Positive, life-giving affirmations build on the understanding that everything is energy, even your thoughts. If you have positive, life-giving thoughts, that energy is sent through your body, to others, and to the universe.

Do affirmations in a quiet place where you will not be distracted. Still your mind by focusing on your breath, a sacred word, or by focusing your gaze at a candle flame or some other object that is optimal for your concentration.

Repeat affirmations slowly and with feeling. If you just repeat them like a broken record without much attention or intensity, they will still help, but the more energy and emotion you put into the affirmation, the more you are energizing the thought form and the more beneficial it will be. So while saying each phrase, put your heart into the affirmation. You might want to add a visualization as well, but feel free to experiment with what works best for you.

If when you are doing affirmations you start to think negative thoughts or feel doubt, skepticism, fear or anger, don't give up, this is normal. You are beginning to find the energy blocks in your thoughts and emotions. Just notice the negative thought or feeling. Then visualize it floating away like a cloud or balloon and begin your affirmation again.

A really powerful time to do affirmations (or visualizations) is at bedtime before you fall asleep. Then while you sleep, the new thought forms will access your subconscious where they will be very effective.

Affirmations and mantras are most effective when they resonate with you personally. It is better to do fewer affirmations that are really powerful for you, than to do many that do not mean much. So find what works for you now and stay with them. After awhile you may need to change them so you can effect transformation at a deeper level. Therefore, I suggest altering them whenever it feels appropriate to do so. Trust yourself!

Chakra

"Chakra" is the Sanskrit word for "wheel," referring to the energy centers in your body that spin like wheels drawing energy from the universe and your own energy fields into your body. There are spiritual meanings and colors generally associated with each of the main chakras. In the affirmation section of each workbook, I list the chakra connected with the message of the chapter, along with its location and color. Focusing on this area and color while you say the affirmations may help you connect with the energy more strongly.

Chakra: Crown/Top of Head
Color: White or Violet

Variations on a Theme: For the affirmation, "I am Light," some other possibilities are

"I am energy."

"I am a divine spark."

"I am Spirit made manifest in a unique and beautiful form."

"I am one with all."

There may be other affirmations that Spirit gives you to use in any given moment. Be flexible and open and receive any guidance with an open and grateful heart.

Write down any new questions, insights, or experiences here.

Further Reading and Study

Harvey, Andrew. *The Direct Path*. NY: Broadway Books, 2000.

Moody, Raymond. *Life after Life*. San Francisco: Harper San Francisco, 2001.

Schwartz, Gary E. with William L. Simon. *The G.O.D. Experiments*. NY: Atria, 2006.

—*The Living Energy Universe*. Charlottesville, VA: Hampton Roads Pub. Co., 1999.

Gerber, Richard. *Vibrational Medicine*. Rochester, VT: Bear & Co., 2001.

Talbot, Michael. *The Holographic Universe*. NY: Harper Perennial, 1992.

Sams, Jamie. *Dancing the Dream*. NY: Harper Collins, 1998.

2

You are Safe

I heard the Divine say, "Tell the people:

"You are always safe. Truly you are. You are always safe.

"The core of you, the Truest Self in you, is Divine Light, so how can you ever be destroyed? Who can harm you? Truly?

"What is Real in you, what is eternal in you, will never die because it has never been born. Therefore, you are always and forever safe. You are always held securely within the Divine Heart.

"Nothing can harm you. You are eternal. You are Light. Therefore, you are always and forever safe.

"When you feel you are in shifting sand, when the ground is shaking, and everything you thought was secure appears to be false, where do you turn?

"Turn to me and return to who you are. Realize you are always within me and I am always in you. You are always in my loving care.

"My Beingness is
Eternal,
Constant,
an ever-abiding Truth.

"This is a ground of being that is always secure, always safe, and always sure. I am Life.

"Let go of your illusion that money, people, jobs, or houses keep you safe and secure. It can all be gone in the blink of an eye. Yet you are still totally safe and secure.

"You are always within my loving care. Be still and know that I am God. You are within this God-Beingness. You are. Therefore, you are safe.

"Security is never to be found in anything material. Security is never to be found in any person or thing. Security is only found in your eternal beingness in the One. This is where you always are. Here you are always safe.

"You may seemingly lose many things, but these things that you can lose are not Real with a capital R. These things, even your body, are all temporary forms of energy, sometimes becoming form, sometimes turning back to energy, from pure consciousness to matter and back again.

"When you know you are eternally secure then no matter what happens to you, you know you are still 'safe.' Safety is not necessarily measured in terms of the earth—physical health, material wealth, lack of abuse and violence, etc. These things cannot create safety, although a sense of safety is necessary for one's well-being. Rather these things are temporary definitions of safety.

"Real safety, real security is in knowing who you are—knowing nothing and no one can ultimately harm you, and knowing the indestructibility of your core self.

"The saying, 'If it doesn't kill you, it will make you stronger' is true. It is even truer from an eternal perspective—'Even if it does kill you, ultimately, it will make you stronger.'

"You are always safe, dear one. Even when it looks like the universe is against you, the universe is for you. The universe is always for you. It supports you, it upholds you, it is working towards your greatest well-being.

"The impediments that come your way may be trying to point you in a new direction you wouldn't have considered without the blocks in your way. The blocks may be helping you go to a deeper level within yourself to heal and to grow.

"When things are falling down around you, whether it is relationships, finances, a job, or loved ones, sometimes things need to come down in order for you to find the True You.

Otherwise, you would cling to your sense of identity and self as connected to people and things. You would identify your self as mother, father, husband, wife, career, salary, house, or child.

"These are not your identity. They are temporary labels and conditions of your temporary dwelling on this earth. The True You is eternal. The True You, the very core of you, is calling you home, to realize that you are always home. The True You is divine, eternal Love and Light in beingness.

"This may inspire some trepidation. Loss of identity! Loss of self! Good God! But you are not losing your Truest Self, only what you think of as self. Disillusionment can be a good thing—you 'dis' your illusions and it is a healthy thing to lose your illusions. Do reality! Be reality!

"Say to yourself every day: 'I am safe. I am always safe. I am always totally loved and totally safe. Thank you for the protection that always surrounds my loved ones and me.'

"Everything that happens is ultimately for the highest and best and nothing happens outside of the Divine Flow and Order. It important for your spiritual maturity to have this level of trust and understanding with *All That Is*.

"It can be very difficult to face these words in dire circumstances or in the midst of a devastating loss or cataclysmic tragedy. Nothing happens outside the Divine Flow and Order? My child died of a surgeon's error, how can that be within the Divine Flow and Order? What about the Holocaust? How is that safety and security?

"Alas, it is one of the most difficult challenges you face. The difficulty is when you look at your circumstances only from a limited perspective. It is perfectly okay to grieve, to be angry, to question, for that is how you move through your emotions and beliefs to come to terms with loss, even your loss of what you think safety is.

"It is part of the journey as well, to seek that such things never happen again. This journey towards peace and away from violence helps raise the consciousness of the entire world into its divine nature, into its own Truest Self.

"Everything is growing and returning to its True Nature. There are many dramas to be played out in the return of all to divine consciousness. Know that in the midst of it all, you are always safe. Know you are always in the abundance of Divine Care.

"When you realize you are always safe, you can play a transformative role, helping everyone you meet, even helping the entire planet!

"When disease, death, financial loss, or violence occur, your sense of safety and even justice may be challenged to their very core. These events can be so destructive and produce feelings of much harm. Indeed, the way of suffering is often the Achilles heel of a person's faith. 'Where were You, God, during this time?

Why didn't You come and rescue me? Why did You allow this to happen?'

"They are valid questions. It is perfectly okay to ask them. You are always held in the arms of Love even when you feel you are completely lost. Even when you no longer believe in anything, you are still within my Beingness.

"If you stay true to the questions and true to yourself in the midst of them, this can also be the way home because these questions drive you to your core to find a deeper truth. No one wants destruction to happen. No one seeks it for themselves unless they are in so much pain it is how they cry out for help or because it seems like the only way out for them.

"But beneath all of the pain is a stronger truth—the truth that you are Light. Beneath all of the fear is a rock of security—the truth that you are always safe. Beneath all of the questioning is a knowing.

"When you have emerged from the other side of a devastating experience, then you can see the help and the healing, the progress and the lessons learned. Pain is a great teacher. Fortunately, you do not have to stay on the path of suffering in order to keep learning, but if a traumatic event does happen to you, you can use it to learn many things. You can even use it to learn that you are always safe, no matter your circumstances.

"You are safe. You are Light. Always.

"Destruction plays a part in the larger cosmos as it reaps a greater healing and wholeness. After experiencing the consequences of destructive actions, individuals and groups, and even countries can rise into a stronger conviction and a higher state of being where such violence is less likely. This happens over and over again in history. The more people who integrate, the more healing can happen to the whole earth.

"So safety does not mean you will avoid challenges, loved one. It is the way of this world that trouble will find you. It is a necessary part of your spiritual progress as individuals, families, communities, and as a species. Integrating and transcending every trying circumstance is the way of maturity.

"When you know and know from the very core of you, that no one is ever lost, that nothing is an accident in the sense that it is meaningless, that there is purpose in it even if you do not yet know what it is, then you realize a different understanding of safety.

"Everyone is beloved. Everyone is a precious form of the Beloved. Nothing and no one is ever lost. You are beloved. You are always safe.

"Your loved ones, you, everyone has come to this earth for a reason and everyone has a purpose. This can be very hard to accept, especially during a time of trial. So, be gentle with yourself. It can take much time and distance from your tragedy to put things into a larger, healing perspective. Allow yourself to heal and to find those who can accompany you on your journey back to wholeness.

"As difficult as it can be to understand in the midst of the challenge, your soul and your loved ones agreed to these experiences prior to your coming to earth in order for you all to learn lessons. Yes, you are safe.

"When you are done here, your life continues uninterrupted in the spiritual realms. You are safe. Your beloved child, mother, or husband is safe on the other side. They are still with you watching over you. You may miss them terribly. You may miss them to the end of your days, but they are safe and you are safe. Your loved ones are always safe, even if they or you are not yet aware of the eternal nature of the soul.

"Even those persons who were killed in great tragedies, many of these souls are living again in new bodies, healing their psychic wounds and helping to heal the world.

"You are always safe—even when everything is falling down around you. You are safe in my loving care. I am with you always.

"When you can detach enough to see the divine drama unfolding—that truly all the world is a stage—and that Eternal Beingness is working out this divine unfolding and re-enfolding through the roles that everyone plays on the earth, then it becomes easier to accept difficult circumstances and to work through them so that all can benefit for their highest purposes.

"When you can stand back and see yourself for the role you are playing, you see the safety that is beneath even the worst atrocities. Within all destructive acts is a divine seed of good. Within all is a holy intention, even if that intention has become warped beyond recognition. Still, the holy within has the final word; is the only Real Word.

"You can always find Light in the darkest places on earth, because it is always there. You can find it because your Truest Self is Light and everyone's Truest Self is Light. Being aware of this Light, you know that you are always safe.

"When you can operate from this secure ground of being, nothing can overwhelm you, and absolutely nothing can throw you. You become a force to be reckoned with, a force to be reconciled with, a great pillar of strength for everyone who knows you and everyone you meet. You become a rock."

I heard the Divine say,
"You are safe. This is always your reality, my loved one."

WORKBOOK
Questions

- How can you feel safe when there is so much violence in the world?

- What is safe?

- When have you felt totally safe? Describe this situation using as many senses as you can: feelings, smells, images, sounds, tastes, etc. As you are transported back to this safe time and place, notice any changes in your body and write them here.

- If you knew with total certainty that you were completely safe all the time, how would your life change?

Meditations

Body Meditation

Repeat this every day and you may even start to believe it! Say it out loud: "I am always safe." Say it like you really mean it. "I am always safe." Go to the safe time and place you described above. Maybe it is a house, or a person, or somewhere in nature. Just go there in your mind and notice how safe you feel again and repeat, "I am safe." Feel your body relax and be at peace.

If you have experienced significant injuries, surgeries, violence, or humiliation, there may be parts of your body that need extra attention and compassion. This is because of "cell memory." Even though you may have healed on many levels, your cells may still remember the trauma and be holding onto it because they do not yet know that you are safe now. Cells have their own consciousness and need to be treated with respect and kindness.

So when you have relaxed your body and are breathing deeply and calmly, lovingly place your hands on one of the parts of your body that has experienced trauma. Send as much love as you can from your heart down through your arms and out your hands into your body. Now you can say to this part of your body, "I am sending you love. You are safe now. You can release the trauma and the memory of the trauma. Release it all now into love and light. You are safe. Thank you for your strength. You can let go now because you are safe. Thank you."

You might "hear" your body talking back to you in protest for what it experienced. That is okay. Just continue to reassure it and talk to your body part and its cells like you would comfort a frightened child. You may have several parts of your body you want to do this for. You can also use this meditation for body parts that are experiencing disease or illness. Imagining white or golden light traveling from your heart through your arms and hands into your body parts can help, too. Then you can say, "I am sending you love and healing light. You can release the illness now." Keep repeating this exercise as much as you need to over many days, weeks, or months. Of course, you can do this along with any traditional medical treatment. Visualizing and meditating right before you fall asleep at night is an especially effective time to meditate because your intentions and visual images sink into your subconscious while you sleep and get worked out at a deep level.

Write down any new questions, insights, or experiences here.

Grounding Meditation

When someone feels safe, they tend to be very grounded. The fight-flight-or-freeze mechanism is turned off and they can just be who they are. People like being around such grounded energy. Here is a meditation to help you.

Sitting or lying down, close your eyes and take several deep breaths into your belly. Feel your body gradually relax. Then imagine in your mind's eye that there are roots growing out of the bottom of your feet and out from your tailbone. Watch these roots continue to grow down into the earth. Gently send these roots all the way to the center of the earth. Just keep going down, down, down. When the roots have reached the center of the earth, then see them spreading into a root system that goes throughout the entire planet.

When the roots are fully-grown, then bring your attention slowly back up the roots and into your body. Focus on your tailbone area, also called the root chakra. You may feel a surge of energy here as your body connects deeply with the earth. If you do not feel anything, that is okay, it does not mean you have not connected. Just continue to say, "I am safe. I am safe. I am always safe." This meditation will help your body know the immense cocooning nature of the earth's energy as well as help your body feel relaxed and safe.

Write down any new questions, insights, or experiences here.

Breathwork Meditation

Breathing properly is one of the best ways to promote your own physical health. It can also help your body feel safe as proper breathing relieves stress, stimulates your energy, and oxygenates your blood. Plus, proper breathing is an excellent way to help heal illnesses.

Breathing into your belly is the proper way to breathe. In our society, too many breathe incorrectly, creating stress and dysfunction in the body. Because our culture's ideal physique includes a flat stomach and six-pack abs we often "suck it in." Unfortunately, this leads to shallow breathing confined to the upper lungs. This does not allow the full intake of oxygen that your body needs to exhale impurities and fight disease.

You can tell if you breathe anatomically correctly, if when you inhale, your belly expands outwards. If instead you find your belly moving inward and your chest outward, you are breathing into your upper lungs only.

Beyond proper, regular breathing, there are many kinds of breathwork that are very good for active, body-based meditations. In cultures around the world, breathwork is a powerful gateway to the Truest Self as it activates intuitive abilities and stimulates the body's own self-healing mechanisms. It is interesting to note that in Hebrew, the word for breath and spirit is one and the same, *ruach*.

There are various types of breathwork. Try them out for yourself and see what works best for you. While you practice breathwork, focus on your breathing and on your body while repeating the mantra, "I am safe. I am always safe."

The Bellows

This breathwork is the belly breath writ LARGE. You inhale through your nose, deep into your belly and exhale through the nose as well. Do several deep breaths very quickly. This can make you dizzy fast, so begin practicing with just a few breaths. The next day you can add another breath-cycle and the next day another and so on until you have worked up to about five-to-ten minutes. Work up gradually and don't overdo! This powerful breathwork is very effective at cleaning the respiratory system rapidly.

The Double Breath

This breathwork is done through the mouth. Take in two inhales and then breathe out with one exhale. It is best if you lie down for this breathwork. The first inhale through the mouth should be a typical belly breath—the belly expands. The second inhale taken right after the first should fill up the upper lungs, expanding the chest. Then exhale through the mouth. This, too, is very powerful, and takes time to build up to. So do no more than 5 minutes at first and then gradually build from there, never doing more than 20 minutes a day. You will find your body extremely relaxed and energized at the same time from doing this breathwork.

Write down any new questions, insights, or experiences here.

Affirmations

Chakra: Root (Tailbone and Feet)
Color: Red

Variations on a Theme: "I am Safe."
"I am grounded."
"I always belong."
"I am always connected to Source."
"Mother Earth is my physical home."
Write down any new questions, insights, or experiences here.

Further Reading and Study

Eden, Donna. *Energy Medicine*. NY: Jeremy P. Tarcher/Putnam, 1998.
    For healing tools related to body meditation, and Triple Warmer meridian work related to sedating the fight-flight-or-freeze response.
Myss, Caroline. *Sacred Contracts*. NY: Harmony Books, 2001.
    —*Anatomy of the Spirit*. NY: Harmony Books, 1996.
    For more explanation of the spiritual meaning of your body's chakras (energy centers).

Other healing books:

Adam. *Intention Heals*. Vancouver, BC: Dreamhealer, Inc., 2008.
    —*The Path of the Dreamhealer*. NY: Dutton, 2006.
Elliott, David. *Healing*. LA: Hawk Press, 2010.
    —*The Reluctant Healer*. LA: Hawk Press, 2005.
Brennan, Barbara. *Emerging Light*. NY: Bantam Books, 1993.
    —*Hands of Light*. NY: Bantam Books, 1987.

3

You are Peace

I heard the Divine say, "Tell the people:

"Be at peace. You are my loved one. I love you more dearly than you are even aware. Be at peace. Be content and free of worry. You are always within my care.

"You are always peace. Always. This is also your True Reality. This is who you are. Peace. Contentment. Not just free of conflict, but full of well-being. Creativity. Fertility. Abundance. Contentment. Fulfilled.

"Be free of anxieties and worries that cloud your mind. They only block your ability to see my loving care in everything. If you see me, you know you are never alone. You are always in my care and I am always in you.

"You are Light. This Light is true peace. Tranquility. Calm. Free of all worry and stress. Can you imagine life without stress? Your body and your life would live out its incredible vitality if you could see through the illusion of worry.

"There is never any need for worry. Whatever tells you that you need to worry is not reality. True Reality is worry-free in total trust and total well-beingness. Be not afraid. You are always in my care. You are always within the sight of my eye. I see you. I know you.

"You are always safe and therefore, you can be at total peace and fully contented, not only with your life, but in every circumstance and with every person.

"Your creativity and your fertility arise out of your sense of contentment. You do not produce effectively from a sense of lack, but only from a sense of abundance and contentment.

"Feel your peace. Feel your contentedness. Find this place within yourself. You may at first feel very restless, anxious, and stirred up, but these are not true to you, these are just things that are attached to you. At your core, you are always peaceful and always content. Find this within you.

"Let go of the chaos, the rage, the fear, the turbulence, the static feelings, and the hungers that drive you away from you. Find the calm. Find the peace. Find the still.

"Peace is a state of mind. It is to not get caught up in the turbulence of your circumstances or the anxiety of your thoughts. Peace is a steady, centered place of the Eternal Beingness within you.

"When you know you do not need anything or anyone outside you to fulfill you, then you have found your True Peace. When you know that you are complete at the core of you, no matter what you feel may lack in your personality or in your circumstances, nothing can draw you off your true path—your path for joining in the creative endeavors of Spirit.

"How can you be fulfilled relationally if you have no partner? How can you be at peace without money? How can you be content when troubles surround you?

"Go within. Go deep within, my beloved one. Find the stillness in the midst of the storm. Do not believe the lies that tell you that you must have these things in order to be peaceful and content. It is not true. These things will only satisfy for a time and then you are hungry and stirred up again.

"Find your true contentment and then you will know the secret of deep peace, of peace that passes all understanding. You will know that all is well, all manner of things is well, all will be well, and all is well. You will know true peace.

"Be at peace. Be content.

"Peace is the ability to transcend any circumstance. Peace is the internal state of oneness with all. When you know you are one with anyone and anything that comes to you, you can stay in your peaceful state and respond without tension, anxiety, fear, lust, or anger.

"Peace is the fruit of meditation. However, not all those who meditate find peace. It is important to know how to use your meditation as a tool and not as an end in itself.

"To use meditation successfully, meditate to find out who you are, not just to experience ecstatic or higher states. Go to the core of you, the center. There is always peace. There is always calm. There is always contentment and fulfillment. Really. If you find this place within yourself then meditation is successful.

"The more you go to that place within, you can find it at any time. You can go there at will in any circumstance, in any place, even surrounded by crowds! Practice this place of peace. Practice going within and being still.

"You are at peace when you know you belong to One and therefore All. You are always home no matter where you are. You always belong no matter what people surround you.

"When you can go there at will and be there at any time, you will bring peace to everyone you meet and every circumstance you are in. Grow and nurture this place within you—this place of knowing, of centered beingness. This is a place of divineness in you.

"Peace is also knowing the illusion of lack. When you know peace, you know the fountain of wellness is there. You know it. You know abundance is within you. You must tap into it like a deep well. You tap into it by going deep, deep, deep within to your place of knowing.

"Peace is a foundation but also a fountain. It builds on the deeper foundation of safety. Knowing you are always safe, you then know you can feel fully at peace. When you are always peaceful you can multiply this reality in the world simply by your presence.

"The peace that is within Me is the peace that is within you.
The peace that can calm a storm.
The peace that passes all understanding.
The deep peace, the void, the womb that is the creative spring-board of all life.

"All is possible in this space. All is safe in this peace.

"From this ground you can grow many fertile, creative projects. From this ground you are always being nourished. You never grow famished. From this ground your creativity blossoms and gives fruit to many. Your abundance grows.

"Like a multi-flowered tree that produces many apples, so is the abundance that is within the universe and within you. Within each apple are many seeds and so one tree can produce an abundance of new trees.

"Of course, not all seeds planted will produce a tree. Birds will eat some seeds, some will blow away in the wind, and not all seeds that bury into the ground will germinate. But those that do grow into a tree will eventually produce many more apples with many more seeds. And so it goes.

"This is the principle you can apply to your own life. You are always in this abundance, whether you experience it or not. In your own life, what fruit are you producing? What seeds are you planting? The key to abundance is to keep producing and keep planting according to who you Truly are. In other words, produce and plant what brings you love, what brings you joy, what delights your soul. Eventually, the fruit and its seed will catch on and produce an abundant harvest.

"Many people think this spiritual principle has to do with money. Intend money, grow money, produce money. But money doesn't grow on trees! Money comes when you are in your truest flow. If material wealth is what you are after then that indeed may come, but perhaps at great cost to your soul.

"Instead, focus on your soul, what feeds your spirit. You will be wealthy spiritually, you will find great wealth, and the material will not matter so much. And you will be provided for. Focus on your spiritual health. Feed your soul and you will thrive. Your work will grow abundantly. Love your work. Do what you love, and the money will follow. This is a true maxim!

"Say to yourself, 'When I follow my bliss, the rest will follow.'

"Of course, you need to know your own bliss. Maybe you have forgotten what brings you true happiness. Maybe you have lost touch with the joy of being who you are. Meditate here. What would you love, love, love to do most right now if you could? This is a key. Ask yourself this again and again. This will create a soul path that will bring you many riches of many kinds...and you will be fulfilled along the way.

"Money is inconsequential on this journey. It may come and then there are responsibilities and blessings in being a channel of multitudinous giving. The money doesn't then belong to you—it is just flowing to you and through you. It may not come in the way that you hope and this too is a blessing, but still the universe provides for you. Spiritually, though, you will be blessed beyond measure. You are blessed to be a blessing. Keep it flowing! Keep your soul growing! Stay in your truest wealth—your Truest Self and you will thrive.

"Abundance flows like grain being poured into your hand. You can only hold so much in your own hand. Everything else that falls through that you cannot hold, gather in a bucket and give it away. This is the principle of abundance: Keep what you need for the day and let the rest go to others. This is the way of the Flow. Every time you try to store for yourself beyond what is needed you begin to build up false security for what is True. Then the lessons with money become harder and harder until you learn this simple truth.

"This does not mean you will have extreme hardship with money, but until these things are integrated, it is important for the money not to flow too much so shadow doesn't overtake it. You then will know what to do with abundance, that is, how much to save, how much to invest, and how much to give away without any worries about the implications.

"You already know this deep within, but as you integrate more and more Light into your consciousness, you will bring your Light to areas of shadow and the abundance will be very clear, pure and bright for you. These can appear to be hard lessons, but it is necessary so that the earth can sustain all forms of life.

"The generosity of your soul comes from the abundance of peace and fulfillment. Knowing you are always provided for and that you have enough, you are able to freely share with those whose circumstances require assistance. Knowing your own value, secure in who you are, you are generous about the value of others who quite simply are you. You see yourself in everyone around you because they are you—the Truest You in different forms.

"Can you live here in abundance, generosity, and peace, no matter where everyone else around you is living? You can. Do not buy into the mirage that tells you that you lack. You do not lack for anything. You have unlimited resources at your disposal. The key is are you living out your Soul's destiny? Are you one with the flow of your life's purpose? Are you being one with the love, joy, and peace you already are at your core? Live here and life will only be full of rich moments."

I heard the Divine say,

"Be at peace, dear one. All is well. Do not worry about your money or tomorrow. All is taken care of. Just be. Just be love.

"You are always peace, loved one. This is your reality. Live in this peace."

WORKBOOK
Questions

• If you were content in your life, what would this mean for you?

• What would it take for you to trust completely that the universe's Flow will support you?

• Where does your creative drive come from?

• Being at peace in your relationships and with yourself requires non-attachment. You do not have false identities about who you are. You are not attached to who you think others should be. You just accept and are at peace. What is your inner guidance telling you about these things in your own life?

- Being at peace in the present means letting go of your past and your future and living in the now. Where are you being invited to let go?

- What brings your soul peace? How can you grow more of this in your life?

- Where do you have abundance already in your life? How can you give from this abundance now?

- What blocks can you identify that are keeping you from feeling peace now? How can you work through and release these blocks?

Meditations

Detachment Meditation

First, repeat this to yourself focusing on your lower abdomen or second chakra. "I am always peaceful. I am always content. Lovingly peaceful. Lovingly productive and creative."

Second, to help yourself detach, visualize cords (like phone cords) going between you and the person or situation you are dealing with. Then visualize unplugging the cords that are attached to the parts of your body that are feeling stressed. There may be several. Just keep unplugging the ends of the cords from your body. Now re-plug these ends into a bright Light above you (God, if you will). Now visualize new cords coming down from the Light and plug them into the voids in your body left by the old cords. That way, you have totally unplugged from the person or situation, you have plugged that person or situation into God, and you have plugged yourself back into God as well.

Write down any new questions, insights, or experiences here.

Clearing Meditation

Find a place to lie down where you will not be interrupted. Breathe mindfully, focusing on your breath and go deep to your center.

Set your intention. "I intend to completely, gently and safely clear _____." Set your boundaries. "Only what is for my highest and best can and will happen."

Ask for guidance and help. "I gratefully ask that God and all of God's ministering beings, angels, and energies assist me in this healing."

Get in touch with what you feel needs to heal. Use as many sensory perceptions as possible. (What does it look like? What color? What shape? What is its substance: gas, solid, liquid, etc. Does it have a smell? A sound? A taste? If you were to touch it what would it feel like?) When you are getting in touch with the color, go to the darkest color you can see—ideally, black.

Once you are in touch with it, you can begin a dialogue with it. Ask it questions. (What are you here for? Why are you in me? What lesson were you here to teach me? Do you always tell the truth?)

Once you feel you have identified it, you then can tell it, "Thank you for helping me and teaching me. However, I've learned the lesson you came to deliver and so I no longer need you anymore." Then tell it to leave. Don't ask; tell or command. It is your body and being and so if you tell it that it must leave, it must. Make sure you are still breathing deeply and well.

To help in this process, visualize God or your Truest Self. For most people this is some form of light. Get in touch with this light or other image that came to your mind. What does it look like? What color? What shape? Continue on with the questions as in the paragraphs above.

Once you have identified the light, then bring this light down into your body wherever you have visualized what needs to heal and see the light dissolving the darkness. Ask God to bring in higher light that is appropriate for you at this time to replace the unwanted energy. This is where the healing might take on a life of its own. The light may start at the top and move down, blanket you, fill you up from inside, explode, or become lightening. Whatever happens is okay.

Continue this process with bringing light in to replace the unwanted energy until it is 100% gone. Continue to tell the unwanted energy to leave. This can happen instantly, over several minutes, a few days or longer. Just stay with the process. If it doesn't leave, it may mean you have some other spiritual lesson to work through for yourself. So just keep at it or find someone who can assist you in this process. Emotions may flow when you are working through this visualization and this is an excellent energy release.

When you feel the unwanted energy has left, or when you feel you have spent enough time with it for the day, end with an open and loving heart. You can also send this loving, grateful energy into your entire body as a refreshing end.

Write down any new questions, insights, or experiences here.

Mirror Integration Meditation

The universe has been programmed to function much like a mirror. Whatever is in your soul is what is reflected back to you. So, the extent to which you embody peace and other divine qualities is what you will experience as you journey through your life. To the extent that you are functioning from a place of lack, fear, anger, etc., the universe reflects that back to you as well, showing you where you need to integrate and learn another spiritual lesson.

How do you know if you have learned the lesson? You know by your lack of reaction to the situation. When you react to someone or some situation, you show that there is a place in yourself that is ill-at-ease (dis-ease) with whatever you have judged in that person or situation. When you do not react, you show equilibrium, balance, and peace. This does not mean that anything goes in other peoples' behaviors. Rather, it means that you can use peaceful avenues to solve your challenges and stay peaceful and detached in and of yourself as you work to meet those challenges.

Look back on the last twenty-four hours or longer and see if you can find someone or something to which you reacted strongly. (That was awful! He is awesome! She was so nasty!) The positive reaction (He is awesome!) might show you that you are not accepting your own awesomeness and are projecting it onto someone else. So, start looking for your own awesomeness and claim it!

Usually, it is the more negative reactions that consume us. The key to healing them in peace is to move away from judging and to move towards compassionate understanding. When you find something you think is negative in someone else, remember to ask, "Where is that in me?" Then take the time to find it in yourself and explore why it is in you. When you feel you are at the core of it, give yourself compassion and forgive yourself. Then you will be able to easily forgive the person you judged. Do this with whatever you found yourself reacting to in the last day or so.

Write down any new questions, insights, or experiences here.

Affirmations

Chakra: Lower Abdomen

Color: Orange

Variations on a Theme: "I am Peace."

"When I practice peace within, more peace is created in the world."

"I am always in abundance."

"I am content."

"I am passionately creative."

"I honor my sexuality."

Write down any new questions, insights, or experiences here.

Further Reading and Study

Nhat Hanh, Thich. *Creating True Peace*. NY: Free Press, 2003.

—*Peace is Every Step*. NY: Bantam Books, 1991.

Carrol, Lenedra J. *The Architecture of All Abundance*. Novato, CA: New World Library, 2001.

Fritz, Robert. *The Path of Least Resistance*. Salem: DMA, 1984.

Palmer, Parker J. *Let Your Life Speak*. San Francisco: Jossey-Bass, 2000.

4

You are Joy

I heard the Divine say, "Tell the people:

"You are always joyful. Always in a state of bliss. Always.

"Your Truest Self is always here. Your present day personality may feel all sorts of things, up and down and all around. But your temporary personality is just temporary. It is not the Truest You.

"Your Truest Self is always in a state of joyful, even ecstatic, bliss. Your Truest Self has never left this state of bliss. This is a place you can go to within yourself.

"This is the joy that has birthed the entire universe. This is the joy of oneness. This is the place where there is never any loss for truly, there is no loss in bliss. All is embraced—all, everyone, and everything.

"Repeat this: 'I am always joyful. I am always in bliss. I am pure joy' while centering on your solar plexus or upper abdomen.

"Bliss is the state of ecstasy. It is sometimes experienced spontaneously in this life. It is a feeling of total oneness and harmony. The infinite universe thrives within it. Bliss is knowing the total happiness and elation at the perfection of all.

"'How,' you may ask, 'is everything perfect when there is so much violence?' Indeed, on this level all is not perfect. Much is tragic. Compassion is given to all those who experience hardship and to all those damaged souls who in soul-ignorance inflict harm to others.

"But from the divine perspective everything plays a part in the re-enfolding of all into Divinity. You may have seen a glimpse of this. When you have experienced bliss, you simply know this is how it is.

"Peace and safety build to joy and bliss. When you know that you and everyone are always safe and when you are always content and know everything at the divine level works harmoniously, then you are open to the joy of the universe, actually the joy of all.

"Imagine you are playing an instrument and you are making many beautiful sounds. When you are playing very well, you begin to become one with the instrument and one with the music. If you are playing music you love, soon you experience the spirit of the melody and music. You become so one with it, you don't notice anyone or anything else.

"The music enraptures you even as you are participating in the playing of it, though it is still larger than you. When you are so enraptured in the beauty of the music, you experience bliss. This is a small example, a small taste of bliss. The more you go along, the more bliss you can experience.

"It is important for you not to rush experiences of Spirit. These come in their own time, in their own way. No, do not seek them, but be grateful for them when they happen.

"Bliss is a state of mind, a state of oneness. It is a place of beauty and harmony. It is the 'all is well' chorus of the Divine. Everyone knows this on some level. Isn't this grand? Yes. You will do well in this life.

"This joy is not from this world, although you can experience it in the world. This bliss is eternal. It is forever, unending and lasting. It does not ride the waves of human ignorance, derision, loss, devastation, or fads. It is not driven by ego or ego desires.

"It is the bliss one sees when a child rides a bicycle for the first time!

"It is the joy of a flower opening to the sun.

"It is the play of the otter, the dance of the stars, the leap of a gazelle.

"It is being and beingness.

"When you are caught up in the joy of creating, of inventing, of writing, the thrill of the moment of life, this touches the bliss within you. Go to this place within you. Go to this place and grow this feeling in you. Then you can be blissful and joyful no matter your circumstances!

"Unbelievable? Maybe, but it is possible. You might temporarily lose it but no matter. You can find it again because it is always there.

"What would change in your life if you were blissful no matter who or what was in front of you?

"Maybe you do not want to try it because it seems too far-fetched. Try it for a time. A few minutes. Then expand your time and see that you can do it at any time.

"Maybe you are really afraid of doing this because it is so powerful your entire life would change! Maybe you are so tied up in drama and suffering (and there is real suffering on the earth) that you think it uncaring to let go of your connection to suffering. Not so!

"You help no one by drowning in their suffering with them. You do not help yourself either if you think you must keep feeling pain in order to have compassion or in order to be a healing presence. These are just beliefs not truths. Let go of your belief that real joy, real bliss is not an ongoing possibility in your earthly life.

"A healer is someone who can stand in the midst of deep suffering, pain, and disease, have total open-hearted compassion for the other, and yet stand grounded and centered in peace and bliss. This is a healing presence. This is possible.

"Joy, deep abiding joy is within you if you are willing to risk everything to find it. Of course, in risking everything, you find that you really have not lost anything. There is no loss in bliss. This is truth. There is no loss in bliss.

"It is often said you must die before you die to advance on the spiritual path. True, but what is death? Nothing more than a shift in awareness. When you are One in bliss, there is never any awareness of loss, only bliss. Try not to attach to such temporary ideas of death. It has such a powerful hold over your culture. There is so much fear of dying.

"Death is just a shift in awareness. Your body is the only thing that expires and even its energy is not lost. All is transformed and recycled into new life. All information is stored. The energy of your soul rises to new life at a new level. You, the True You, continue on as if you have just awoken to a bright new day. Try not to buy into the fear of death and the many fears associated with it: aging, disease, and loss of vitality.

"Joy is your birthright. Joy is your natural state of being. It is not unnatural to be joyful. Rather, it is unnatural not to be! The reason people are not joyful is because they are encumbered by things they are unaware of that are dragging them down. So many things can drag down joy: worries, fears, attachments, needs, losses, grief—many, many things.

"Joy cannot be manufactured—you cannot force joy. Rather you uncover joy. Joy is to be found underneath all the layers of heaviness that trap the bliss at the core of your being. To find joy, you let go of everything else and just go to joy. Joy is already there. All you have to do is release the baggage. Travel light and light-heartedly. Joy travels well with these companions.

"Joy is such a blessing, my beloved one. It is a gift you can give to yourself and to others. It shines in the darkest places. It brings light to the dreariest corners on the earth. Joy will help to heal you and to heal your loved ones and your planet. Joy is the fullest expression of your core star. Joy is the foundation of love. They work hand in hand. When you know joy, you find love. When you love, you know joy.

"When you know the bliss of oneness, the joy of unity, you also know your infinite value. Can you embrace your own worth? You may feel small and insignificant. Or, you may only feel you have value if other people tell you this, or if you have an important job or a lot of money. But your innate value has nothing to do with the value of your work or with the value you are perceived to have by society, or even your feelings. You are valuable just for who you are.

"Your value is in your beingness, not your doingness.

"You are more valuable to me than I can describe to you. You are more valuable to all, to the whole, than you can even imagine. You are a part of me and I, you. This is always true, regardless of your thoughts and feelings about yourself.

"When you can embrace your own worth, you can embrace the value of every facet of nature, every person you see, of all. You can love yourself freely. This comes very easily when you first realize the oneness of all. When you know that all is a divine manifestation interconnected in a beautiful array of light, like a woven intergalactic garment where even the smallest thread is of fundamental importance to the overall design and crafting of the whole, you know your own infinite value.

"Each person and each atom play a part. None are lost to my sight. When you know your worth and the worth of all, you are rich in joy. You know nothing is ever lost. You know who you are. You can live in joy regardless of your up and down feelings and over time your feelings begin to balance and you can live continually in the Presence of joy.

"Joy leads to praise, praise to joy: an ecstatic circle celebrating the dance of oneness. Expand your consciousness. Become one with all. Open to all. This is pure bliss."

I heard the Divine say,

"Be not afraid. You are going to be okay. Everything will be all right, my beloved one.

"Stay in the place of joy. Be joyful. Be."

WORKBOOK
Questions

• Describe a time of great joy in your life. What were you feeling, thinking, seeing, hearing, experiencing? What was meaningful about this time?

• If everything you needed was provided for, for the rest of your life, how would you spend your time?

• If you could give one gift to the world that would give you the greatest joy, what would it be?

- How do your answers to these questions, point you to your bliss and your divine purpose?

- Where do you feel joy in your body? You can give yourself this feeling at any time. Just imagine that you have whatever it is that brings you joy, allow yourself to feel the joy it would bring you, and then carry this feeling around in your body as long as can throughout your day. If you forget, do not worry, just bring back that feeling into your body. What differences do you notice in your day? Your mood? Your circumstances?

Meditations

Nature Meditation

In a previous chapter I had you imagine that you are one with anyone in front of you. In bliss you can experience that oneness. Choose a tree that you love. It could be one that is in your yard, or one that you played on when you were a child, or a tree you pass every day on your way to work. Go again to that quiet place inside and breathe to calm yourself. In your mind, imagine the tree, or if you can see the tree, gaze intently at it and then ask its permission to become one with it. If you feel you received a yes in some form, then proceed. If you feel you received a no, choose another tree or wait until another time to try again.

If you received a yes, then either in your mind or while gazing at the tree, set your intention to become one with the tree. This is all that you need to do. It will begin to happen at the level of which you are capable. As your energies merge, you may "feel" the tree. You may "hear" the tree speak to you in some form. What does it have to teach you about joy or any other quality of your Truest Self? If you would like, you can tell the tree whatever you want and listen for a response.

Write down any new questions, insights, or experiences here.

Body Prayer

A body prayer is a great way to unlock joy in your physical being. Choose one of your favorite poems, scriptures, song lyrics, psalms, or another writing that inspires you. Then think up body motions to go along with the meanings of the words, phrase by phrase. When you are ready, you can slowly read the words aloud with meaning, acting out the body motions as you go. Repeat this again as a prayer to Spirit. What did you experience in your body? Your soul?

Write down any new questions, insights, or experiences here.

Affirmations

Chakra: Solar Plexus or Upper Abdomen
Color: Yellow

Variations on a Theme: "I am Joy."

"The universe always provides for me when I surrender to the highest and best."

"I love myself unconditionally."

"I have infinite worth."

"There is no loss in bliss."

"My Truest Self is always in bliss."

Write down any new questions, insights, or experiences here.

Further Reading and Study

Beck, Martha. *Steering by Starlight*. NY: Rodale, 2008.

— *The Joy Diet*. NY: Crown Publishers, 2003.

Barks, Coleman, trans. *The Essential Rumi*. San Francisco: Harper, 2004.

The premier Sufi poet on ecstasy and bliss.

Campbell, Joseph. *The Power of Myth*. NY: Knopf Doubleday Publishing Group, 1991.

Author of the phrase "follow your bliss."

The Dalai Lama with Howard Cutler. *The Art of Happiness*. NY: Riverhead Books, 2003.

5

You are Love

I heard the Divine say, "Tell the people:

"You are Love. At the core, your heart is intimately one with the Divine Heart. Your true heart is my heart: all the compassion, all the love, unbounded and free. It knows only love, for you are this love. This is who you truly are. You are love.

"Being the love that you are is the central task of your journey. Without love, all becomes shallow, just empty chatter and gonging bells with no melody.

"Love grounds all your activities in the being of God's beingness. Love roots your thoughts and feelings and actions so that they are at one with the Divine flow and order.

"Love is.

"When you open your heart to Love, you open your heart to the universes and beyond. The universes exist in love. Love is greater than the universes.

"Love is God's only intention. How can this be? Especially with war and violence, and the tragedy that befalls everyone at some time on the earth?

"Because love is within all. You can find love within a tiny seed. The shadow of ignorance over your planet is burning off and will burn off in the fires of love.

"By immersing yourself in the fire of love you help to heal your planet of its unawareness and bring the seed of love that is within all, even shadow, to full flower and fruit.

"Your planet can be saved. There is time. There is always time. Be in love. Exist in love. Immerse yourself in love. Do not seek for anything or anyone else. Just love. Be love.

"Dwell in the immense sea, float in the immense ocean of love that swells around all, in all, and through all.

"When you consciously dwell in love, not like a fish in the sea because it is not conscious of the water it exists in, but when you dwell in love consciously with your whole mind and attention, not distracted by thoughts or interruptions that take you away from your ever-abiding reality, you flow like a mighty river. You create a swell of love within all those you meet and all those who come in contact with you.

"Dwell in this love every moment. Feel your heart open to its greatest capacity and still you will find that the heart can grow more. It can expand to infinite capabilities. Infinite love. Do you feel your heart growing, enlarging, expanding? Yes, this is your confirmation that it is happening within you. Open your heart to feeling love, too.

"Feel compassion, but don't stop there. Ground all your thoughts, perceptions, ideas, and actions in love. Ground all your feelings in love. Go to love first before you react with an emotion such as anxiety and anger.

"Love is true. Anxiety and anger and even grief are illusions. You can go to love first. Then all your words and actions will flow from love. Catch yourself before you speak even one word of criticism or malcontent. Then go to love and see how that transforms your words.

"It is important that all your intentions be love. Say, 'I am always love; everything I think and do and say comes from love.' Feel this with your whole heart when you say this.

"Love with all your being. Love with all your heart. Do this and you will live your truest life.

"Do not withhold this love from anyone. Love even the least of these. Love even those you cannot stand! How do you do this? By finding within yourself the part of them you dislike. Then come to understand why it is in you and bring forgiveness and compassion to that part of yourself. Then you will be able to love even the enemy.

"Love is not bound by anything. Love is unlimited for everyone. Every creature, too, is cherished and has a place in the overall flow and order.

"Love is simply knowing the infinite value of the person in front of you—knowing it, feeling it, thinking it, and acting on it.

"This love is full. It does not dry up ever. It is eternal. It does not go away. Love is the nature of God. It is the very fabric of the universe.

"Dwell in this ever-abiding love. Try to feel it all the time. Can you? It is a stretch at first but soon your whole being will love living in the feeling of love. You will thrive, as will those around you.

"Love is brilliant and majestic. It makes plants grow, flowers blossom, people heal. Love is life. Love is what you are learning, what you will learn. The ebb and flow of life opens the door to love.

"It will flow through you at all times. You will be love.

"When you are swimming in love, then you know nothing else matters. You will know what you need to know, and receive what you need to receive. You will be in the Divine Flow and Order so that you will know the indestructibility of your essence.

"Feel love, think love, speak love. Say to yourself: 'I am always loving and compassionate to all.' Feel this strongly in your heart when you say it. Say it silently and say it out loud. Say it until you feel it.

"Just one drop of this love is enough to completely heal your heart and soul and the same is true for everyone.

"Love is who you are. The more you dissolve everything that is not love that has attached itself to you, the more you reveal the love you already are. Dissolve everything in love. Dissolve everything in compassion. It all dissolves in love: all the hatred, all the poison, all the fear, all the negativity, all the destructive thoughts and actions.

"Love and compassion set people free to be who they are. It may not be who you want them to be, or even who they want to be, but compassion is the open door to the Truest Self.

"You never have to worry for you live in the Divine Love that is within you and within the entire universe.

"Love blossoms like a rose, but it never fades. Love is an eternal rose of beauty you can always turn to within yourself. If you have love, you don't need anything. You are home. You are yourself. You are. Because you love, you are. Say this affirmation, 'I Love, therefore I am.'

"Love flows like a mountain river—always moving, always flowing, always available—the never-ending fountain of life."

I heard the Divine say,

"You are my beloved. You are my love. You are love. Live in this love and your life will blossom like the rose."

WORKBOOK
Questions

• When have you received limitless or unconditional Love? What effect did that have on you?

• When have you given limitless or unconditional Love? What effect did that have in your life?

• What prevents you from living in this Love all the time?

- How can you grow in this Love?

- If your Truest Self is limitless Love, how does that change your image about yourself? How would it change your life? Your work? Relationships? Your mood?

- How is "God is Love" real to you?

Meditations

Open Heart Meditation

Find a quiet place where you will not be disturbed and lie down or sit in a comfortable position. Breathe deeply into your center. Put your hands over your heart, sending love to yourself. Set your intention to give and receive limitless love. Visualize your heart's energy as a bright emerald green or warm rose that surrounds your heart. Feel the warmth, the light, and the love that are there for you. It may help to focus on someone or something you love, whether a person, pet, or part of Nature.

When you feel strong in this love, visualize the healing light around your heart grow until your entire body is within this heart light. Notice how your body feels. When you feel ready, grow this heart light again until the building you are in is completely surrounded by and immersed in this light. Continue gradually expanding this warm, loving light so your neighborhood, then city, state, country, and finally the entire planet are within this limitless love. Hold this awareness in your heart as long as you would like, then gradually visualize the light returning to your heart. Give gratitude to Spirit for the opportunity to grow love within yourself and the world.

Write down any new questions, insights, or experiences here.

Active Love Meditation

Sending Love (the limitless, no-strings-attached kind) can be one of the most rewarding and joyful experiences of life. This is an active meditation, meaning you can do it throughout your day. It is still meditation, though, as it requires mindfulness.

To help increase awareness of your active meditation, choose something to carry with you or put in front of you. It could be a small stone, favorite amulet, charm, flower, picture, or talisman.

You can place this item in your pocket, so every time you put your hand in it, you remember to be aware. Or, you can place it on your desk, dashboard, mantle, or windowsill—wherever it will capture your attention the most throughout your day.

Whenever you see this item, remind yourself to return to the Lover you are and to send this Love out into the world. Send Love out to the grocery store clerk as this person hands you your receipt. Send Love to your co-workers as you sit beside them in a meeting. Send Love to your food as you prepare it for your family for dinner. Send Love out through your emails and through your voice over the phone. Send Love to your family members as you hug and say hello or good-bye. Send Love out to other drivers on the road. Send love to the birds and animals and trees and earth as you take a walk. Wherever you go, no matter what you are doing, whenever your Love charm gets your attention, send Love out to the world.

Write down any new questions, insights, or experiences here.

Affirmations

Chakra: Heart

Color: Green

Variations on a Theme: "I am Love."

"I am always totally and unconditionally loved."

"I am compassionate in thoughts, words, and actions."

"I and the Beloved are One."

"I am always within the Sacred Heart. The Sacred Heart is always within me."

Write down any new questions, insights, or experiences here.

Further Reading and Study

Ladinsky, Daniel. *Love Poems from God*. NY: Penguin, 2002.

Feinstein, David, Donna Eden, and Gary Craig. *The Promise of Energy Psychology*. NY: Jeremy P. Tarcher/Penguin, 2005.

Levine, Stephen. *Healing into Life and Death*. NY: Anchor Books, 1987.

Orloff, Judith. *Emotional Freedom*. NY: Harmony Books, 2009.

Nhat Hanh, Thich. *Anger: Wisdom for Cooling the Flames*. NY: Riverhead Books, 2001.

Zukav, Gary and Linda Francis. *The Heart of the Soul: Emotional Awareness*. NY: Simon and Schuster, 2002.

Emoto, Masaru. *The Hidden Messages in Water*. Hillsboro: Beyond Words Publ., 2004.

6

You are Truth

I heard the Divine say, "Tell the people:

"You are truth. You are always abiding in truth. You are always free to speak and express who you truly are.

"You can repeat this to yourself: 'I am truth. I am always free and safe to speak my truth in love.'

"Is there absolute truth? Yes, but no one has access to it in its totality. Everyone has an angle on truth like a multifaceted jewel is absolute but has many facets and faces.

"Always speak the truth, your own truth in love, so that others might hear it and see another facet of the jewel that is the ultimate truth. So many of you have been harmed for speaking truth in the past. Much healing must happen here.

"For some the lesson is to learn when to speak truth and when to be silent. For others it is how to speak one's truth in love. Yet for others it is a slow process to learn to speak one's truth at all. Still others are learning how to speak their truth without saying a word!

"This truth is healing even if it at first might feel painful. It is important to be willing to let go of your attachments and allegiances to the limited truth so you can embrace larger and larger visions of truth.

"Be compassionate with all on their journey. Everyone learns at the right pace and at the right level for them.

"Sometimes people cannot hear your truth, though sometimes you must speak anyway. Sometimes you must keep speaking but always in love. Do not lose your voice, your truth. It is essential to the health of all. Be discerning and wise. Do not keep your truth in silence if your truth needs air, light, and room to heal, to grow, and to express itself. You may find creative ways to express who you are. When some ways seem shut to you, other ways open up.

"Truth needs light and love to grow into a healthy outgrowth. Truth blossoms when love is flowing. Truth must be grounded in love or it grows brittle.

"Do not fear. Truth is strong. Even when it is hidden, truth is there, ever-growing and ever-expanding. Truth does not go away.

"Truth is not merely the absence of lies. It goes beyond an absence of dishonesty. Real Truth is full of beauty, full of life, full of well-being. Truth is more than honesty, though that is a necessary ingredient. Truth shows up wherever there are life, light and love. They are not separated though distinguished.

"Truth flourishes when you know you are safe. When all know they are safe. Open to all truth within yourselves. Open to all truth. This is a path and a process, not an instant all-knowing. Truth is communicated through your whole being—your energy speaks even when you remain silent.

"In time you will come into the truth of your entire beingness. You will be at home in your own self so that truth can light the way through your communication and through your entire being.

"Truth is always there. Say: 'I am always truth. I am always loving and truthful. I am a vessel, an instrument of truth, of divine truth.' Yes. Truth is multi-faceted. It shines like a gem through the facets of each individual truth that together reflects the infinite truth of all.

"Truth flows like a river spreading light to those you comfort in speech, in writing, in action. Speak your truth, but live your truth. Be your truth. Be truth. Not in a rigid sense of true vs. false, but truth in an expansive, ever- growing light—like a lantern that grows larger until the dark is consumed in all light. This is truth. It lights the way for others.

"Your truth' can be a bit confusing. Some people by saying, 'Stay true to your truth' mean relative truth, their own story. But what happens? His truth and her truth and their truth and our truth and my truth are all fragments. This is ego truth that can divide.

"There is a larger truth that is true of all that does not divide but acknowledges unity. Stay true to this Truth, that each of you is a ray of the divine sun, unique and yet one. The larger truth is Love. Truth without the all-encompassing, ever-present Love is defensive and ego-based.

"Try not to reduce truth to your side of a story, or even your story. Your story is just a chapter in a book that you've written, but you are not the story, you are not the chapter, you are not the book you are writing. Who are you then?

"Although you are in the story too, the Truest You is outside the story—authoring, watching, learning, growing, creating, loving. The Truest You is journeying into theosis, union with God. The Truest You in actuality has never left. It is just your awareness that is growing back into theosis.

"In awareness you are continually connected but most of your awareness is hidden in shadows, in sub-consciousness. In the manifestation of time and space, all will come to the light and you will see yourself for who you are. Then you will grow into ever-expanding states of awareness and you will know, reaching into infinity, into the farthest stretches of the mystery.

"This is truth. You are truth. You are beloved. This is beauty in its purest form. Truth is beauty personified in you.

"Truth shines through all. Truth is who you are. Truth is not whom you attach to, your body, your emotions, your thoughts, your name, reputation, or your history. None of these is who you really are. You are a bright morning star. All are. This is the truth that shines in you and through you and through all.

"Truth expands with the Light so that there is ever more to learn and to know. There is no stasis; there is no stagnancy in the Divine. There is an eternity to learn and an infinite amount to study. No need for worries there! So much to learn, so much to be, so much to become.

"When you speak, always try to speak gently. Sometimes a forceful word is necessary, but in general try to speak without the energy of force. It is more useful for conveying the messages of love and light.

"Of course, this is done when you speak from your open heart of compassion. When you speak from here, you open the voice to the vibrations that carry healing and truth. When you connect your voice to your heart you open the floodgates to channel the divine word to others.

"So when you speak, speak from your open heart. This takes great mindfulness and presence. This is a task as arduous to accomplish as any mindfulness practice but it reaps great joy in you and all those around you.

"It resonates with all of creation, sending vibrations of love out into the world that help raise all to their core, their origin, their Truest Self. It resounds like a mighty chorus in the universe, singing with rocks and trees, birds and bees, and all manner of manifested things. When you speak from love or sing from love, this is the hallelujah within all. This is where to live: in love, joy, peace, and truth.

"Sing from the depths! Speak from an open heart! Live your Truth!

"Believe in the divine truth no matter what the circumstances appear to be. Circumstances are ephemeral. Divine truth is everlasting. When you can stand in the divine truth no matter what, you are one with the faith that can move mountains, calm a storm, and raise the dead to new life. Believe in my word more than your own life. Trust in what you know at the very core of you.

"I am there. Your Truest Self is also there. We are together in a divinely intricate dance that burns in eternal flames of passionate embrace—a unity that defies all reason, a oneness that you can know and experience but rarely explain. Language is too limited. So use the tools of dance, of art, of poetry, of play, of paradox, of humor, to portray the eternal truth that goes beyond the limits of human understanding. Yes, here is where we always are together, my beloved.

"This is the truth behind all forms: your body, plants and animals, to the earth and the Sun.

"Stand in your Truth. Dance it. Speak it. Sing it. Portray it. Write it. Be it.

"Truth has so much to do with integrity. If you can be honest with yourself, you can see and therefore integrate your shadow. The more truthful in love you are with yourself, knowing your thoughts, feelings, intentions and actions, the more you receive pure, clear results from your intentions. Your integrity or your oneness—no one can take this away from you. Your truth—no one can take this away from you. It is always there in beauty and love and wholeness.

"Truth is the integrity to be completely clear about your intentions. Truth is to say what you mean from an open heart of love with highest intentions. Truth is the strength of character to act on one's word. Truth is to be who you are, to be honest about who you are, and open to all facets of yourself in light and shadow.

"If you mean what you say and say what you mean, from a compassionate heart and soul, your words have incredible power for healing and growth. This honest intentional compassionate speech is the basis for trust and relationship. Without it, no one truly knows who you are.

"Speaking from your core produces much fruit for love and light. Speak from deep peace. Speak from an open heart. Speak from the joy that never dies and is always flowing. Speak from light.

"Truth and integrity are one. Without truth one cannot have integrity or be integrated. Self-distance helps here. It is important to be able to observe one's self in a detached manner. This enables your Truest Self to consciously interact and work through your present-day personality bringing what is in the sub-conscious into the conscious and what is in shadow into light.

"Self-honesty brings this about: watching and observing one's thoughts, feelings, and actions as you would watch and observe another person. There is no need to judge one's self, just a wise discernment that can be honest and forthcoming. This takes time to develop.

"One must first have a strong sense of self to do this—a strong sense of self-value and worth. Some people are still working on building up their self-worth to a point that they can look at themselves very honestly. To look that honestly at themselves now would harm the little self-esteem they have. This hopefully happens in the younger years, but for some who have been disenfranchised, it may take into the adult years for self-worth to arise. Then a conscious spiritual path can be embarked on that includes an ability to take an honest self-assessment of one's inner life. So many people rush around, taking absolutely no time for self-assessment. Honest, compassionate self-assessment is vital to advancing on the spiritual path.

"This is the truest word; be of good cheer. Be not dismayed. Be of the light of all. Be a shining beacon so others may see and become the light and truth that they are."

I heard the Divine say,

"Blessings, blessings, and no worries, my beloved.

"You are truth. Be truth. Be the truth that you are. You are Beloved!"

WORKBOOK
Questions

- What does Truth mean for you?

- With whom or in what places do you feel safe to speak your Truth?

- How do you like to express your Truth through play and creativity?

- If you were always safe to speak your Truth in love how would this impact your life?

- How are Truth and Beauty connected?

- How can you hold your truth in love and stay open to receiving new truth?

Meditations

Sacred Reading Meditation

This meditation is traditionally called *lectio divina*, which in Latin means "sacred reading." Take a small portion of a text you want to focus on. It might be a poem, a scripture or some other inspired writing. Read it through slowly, gently, and meditatively. You may want to read it through one or more times to let its essence sink into your soul.

After you feel that you have connected with the text, reflect on its significance to you at this time. What is it saying to you?

What jumps out at you? What words or phrases have an emotional pull for you? Repeat them slowly, pondering what they mean for your life right now.

When you feel you have received a sacred message for you personally, respond in some way to what you have heard. You may want to write in your journal, paint, create a poem, or take a walk repeating the words that had power for you with each step; whatever feels would be the best for you at this time.

Following your response take some time to just rest in what you have received from this reading. *Lectio divina* can be done in a few minutes or stretched out over a weekend retreat, but the process is the same: read, reflect, respond, rest.

Write down any new questions, insights, or experiences here.

Chanting Meditation

Chanting and singing as forms of meditation are powerful. By invoking the voice, you add audible vibration to your intentions and thoughts and thus, strengthen them. You are also aligning your body and its energy to healing energy vibrations in the universe. Additionally, your vocal vibrations help to open the throat chakra as well as other chakras.

Interestingly, the words used by various traditions for chanting can sound very similar: ah-om, ah-men, and ah-ho. There are various theories why these particular sounds are effective. But whatever sounds and words you use, the most important aspects of chanting are intention and focus.

For chanting, choose whatever word or words you would like to use. Begin chanting at a speed and a tone that are comfortable for you. While part of the significance of chanting is repetition in speed and tone in order to help induce a meditative state, feel free to experiment with pacing and intonation. Using different tones will produce unique vibrations that resonate with particular chakras and body parts. If instead you choose to sing, be aware of the vibrations you feel in your body when you sing different notes. Use this vibration as a healing tuning fork, sending the vibration to the rest of your body and out to the world. Dance and do motions while you sing if this helps you connect with the intention and vibration of the words and music.

Whatever you do, whether chanting or singing, do not worry about how it sounds. Begin by yourself if you have never vocalized in front of groups. Your chanting and singing will get stronger over time. At first you might want to do this along with a chanting or meditative singing CD to help you learn how to free your throat's energies and help release your mind and body to the freedom of expression that is within you.

Write down any new questions, insights, or experiences here.

Affirmations
Chakra: Throat
Color: Sky Blue
Variations on a theme: "I am Truth."
"I am safe to express my truth in love."
"I am open to receiving all Truth in love for my highest and best."
"I am free."
"I am free to express my Truest Self fully."
"I speak and sing from Love."
"I am free to choose how I will express myself moment by

moment, day by day."

Write down any new questions, insights, or experiences here.

Further Reading and Study

O'Neil, Sally & Suzanne Seaton. *Pilgrimage of the Soul*. Freeland, WA: Soaring Eagle Publ., 2004.

Wilber, Ken. *Integral Spirituality*. Boston: Shambhala, 2006.

— *A Theory of Everything*. Boston: Shambhala, 2000.

Leonard, Linda Schierse. *Meeting the Madwoman*. NY: Bantam Books, 1993.

Estes, Clarissa Pinkola. *Women Who Run with the Wolves*. NY: Ballantine Books, 1992.

Rummet, Hillevi. *Pathways of the Soul*. Victoria, BC: Trafford, 2006.

7

You are Wisdom

I heard the Divine say, "Tell the people:

"Wisdom is truth used exceptionally well. Wisdom is more than perception; it is perception through the eyes of love.

"Focus on your sixth chakra in your forehead. Say, 'I am always wise in my perceptions, always loving in all my thoughts.'

"Many seers who can perceive great things are not necessarily wise or loving, so focus on wisdom and loving here. Wisdom is the ability to see and understand, and have compassion and know what one's response is to be.

"Wisdom is a mature knowing. It has the free heart of love as a child, but it has the clear understanding of an adult, too. Wisdom sees and knows and believes and is.

"Wisdom is who you are. You must find it within yourself. Many are smart but not wise. Others have their hearts open but trip when it comes to loving with wisdom. See with and through the eyes of the heart and have an understanding wisdom. This does not mean judging. It means knowing with compassion. It means acting and responding for the highest and best of all to the best of your abilities.

"Wisdom of the highest order comes from love. Wisdom and perception are distinct. Intuitive seeing and hearing, or clairvoyance and clairaudience, are skills that are not necessarily tied to spiritual advancement. Some use these for ego advantage, just like a skilled musician might not use their gifts to benefit others, but for fame only.

"Wise perception is based on love. To use perception wisely is to be clear about one's own shadow, to have only the others' highest and best in mind, to have only love in your heart, to not be worried about money or what other people think of you. In other words to be free of ego concerns of the limited self.

"Wisdom knows when to speak and when not to, knows how to speak, knows what to speak.

"Wisdom knows all is well and all will be well. Wisdom believes all is possible.

"Wisdom sees there is a pattern, a flow, a design where everything is perfect and perfected in love.

"This wisdom embraces mystery; knowing as well as unknowing. You know what you know AND you know all still dwells in mystery. Humility is an important component of wisdom.

Everyone is learning. Everyone is a student. Everyone is growing at the right pace for them.

"Hold your knowing loosely, not too rigidly. Hold it lightly, not too seriously. This is true wisdom. Your beliefs have changed before. Be open. They may change again! Your paradigms can always shift into greater understandings of wisdom.

"Holding knowing and unknowing together makes life free and full of play. Be open to surprises from Me. Be open to the new, the unexpected, the adventure. Be wise and confident in your knowing, and yet do not attach your identity, self-image, or security to it.

"Be willing to let it all go if Love shows you a different way. Hold all knowing and unknowing in compassion. This, too, is true wisdom.

"You are always held in loving wisdom. I know, my beloved, what fears and traumas keep you blocked and hidden behind walls and masks of seeming security. There is no condemnation. There is only my Love that can transmute your fears into pure gold.

"The manifold mysteries of the universe and beyond are a delight for those who know the Love that dissolves all fear. Release your need for control. Dwell in the ever-present Now with me. Open to the Play of all Reality. Past, present, and future—there is no need for fear. In the highest wisdom, all is dissolved in Love. All pain. All fear. All suffering. All. It all plays a part. Love lifts all into ever-present awareness.

"Blessed be the total wisdom that runs and flows through all. Blessed be the grace that heals all. Blessed be the rich river of love that seeks to bring all into One. Blessed are you, my beloved one. You are always held in my wisdom.

"You know the One. You see the One, you feel the One. You are a part of the One; the whole that knits together the strands of time and place into a beautified garment of blessing of the One whose mind has projected all.

"Blessed be the One who weaves fragments into a unified whole of joyful design. Be One. Be in the One. Be in the flow of One. This is wisdom: to seek to be flowing without resistance. Manifested reality is malleable. You will learn of this.

"There is a scripture: 'The wisdom coming down from above is first of all pure, then peaceable, gentle, willing to yield, full of compassion and good fruits, without a trace of partiality...' In other words, wisdom walks through the other chakra energies. It is important to work on all the chakra energies, integrating all into wisdom. These qualities show you have integrated and know wisdom.

"You are this wisdom already, although it takes time to live into this Reality. This wisdom of Reality knows the infinite possibilities. This wisdom knows that in Love all is possible. Nothing is set in stone. There is always hope, for all is possible. In wisdom, you can hold all within the space of hope.

"You are this wisdom. You are beloved.

"Wise action is sometimes a challenge because so many other things can interrupt clear intentions. You may react to a situation or a person emotionally with stress or anger or mentally with harsh thoughts. These can be purified and cleared so that in every situation you learn to respond from your Truest Self, from the place of deep wisdom within you.

"When you are in the present moment, when you are in your Truest Self awareness, nothing can cause you to act in a way that is not wise and loving. Everything you think and say and do will be from a deep knowing and a clear seeing. You will be the wisdom you are.

"You are wise—wise beyond your wildest imaginings. Your genius resides here. Everyone is a genius of something, reflecting the magnitude of the Divine's manifold and manifested wisdom. You are a facet of this magnificence, this bright jewel of wisdom. You are. You are never separated from this wisdom, though at times you may feel you are.

"This wisdom is all-knowing and all-seeing and you can tap into this. This all-knowing and all-seeing aspect of the Divine is vast beyond any one person's comprehension but it is still there and you are a channel of it as everyone is.

"Do not feel that you are unworthy of the Divine. All are worthy. All are Divine. All are my children. It may take a long time for some people to realize this. When they do, they come into alignment with their Truest Self and they become wise.

"Yes this is so. You are wise for you reflect and are the wisdom of Spirit.

"When you live in the vast possibilities you live in the place of miracles. It is important to first understand that circumstances are not Reality. Circumstances are never Reality. Circumstances are like the props on a stage. They are only real for the scene and the characters the actors are playing. But the props: the furniture, backgrounds, and various stage pieces are not Real. You are not really looking at someone's living room or at an ocean on stage. You are not really watching the wind blow through the trees on stage. These are all artificial props to help you imagine that you are there and to help you imagine that these things are happening so that you can follow along with the story of the play.

"This is how to view the circumstances of your life if you want to be free and live in the wisdom of the vast possibilities. The circumstances in your life are just props. Not Real with a capital R. Even the people you know are simply forms of the Beloved. Certainly they are forms in physical matter, but still it is their essence that is eternally Real, not their physical forms. Their physical forms are just energy in dense form. If you remember to view your circumstances from this perspective, it will be much easier to stay detached from the drama that unfolds around you.

"Everything that happens is helping you learn lessons on becoming more and more unified with Spirit. It is just an unfolding drama. The drama helps you learn, it has a drop of measured reality to it, but overall, the drama is not Real. Of course, you still interact in the drama, you still have a role to play in the drama, and you are learning as you go.

"But just like an actor knows on some level while he or she is acting that this is not really who they are, that it is a temporary role they have taken on, and that it is not Real, so too, you can view your life from this perspective. Thus, when trials or joys come, you can say, 'This is just the drama of the play I am in. Who I really am is watching and observing the unfolding drama, learning, growing, expanding, and integrating.'

"What this also means is that when you are watching the drama of the circumstances unfolding around you, you do not have to attach any of your self-worth, your security, your peace, joy, love, and truth to these circumstances. You can remain who you Really are in the midst of the circumstances.

"When you can remember this, when you can see the props for what they are, then it is much more likely that you will be able to alter the props. What I mean by this is that you can literally move mountains when you know the true nature of the mountain. You are not deceived by the transient nature of the physical reality. You know the infinite possibilities that can be in any given moment. You know that at any time, the stage manager in the play can get up and go and move the furniture around. You can even talk to the stage manager and consult with the stage manager about any manner of changes to the props in the play.

"This is different than the self-determination of your culture. This is knowing Reality, knowing the infinite possibilities, and working with the Flow of Reality to help people and the universe heal into Reality. Your ego will try to get what it thinks you want and need. Your Truest Self is free of all want and need and lives in the already manifested abundance of Joy, Love, Truth, and Wisdom.

"Remain in this place of infinite possibilities, knowing that anything can change at any time. This is where true wisdom and true freedom live. There are no worries here. You become one with the mind of Reality, the heart of Love, the wisdom of all.

"The infinite possibilities may seem like a dream world, but it is more Real than anything you can see in the physical world. The physical world is a matrix, the grid of consciousness that allows people to work out their lessons in the dramas and plays of their lives. When they awaken and remember who they are, then the drama and play continues, but the actors have remembered that they are not really the characters in the play and that makes all the difference.

"This is a challenging and exciting place to live one's life! In the world, but not attached to it. So no matter what travails and sufferings befall you, beloved one, you are not beholden to buy into what the world says you should be thinking, feeling, and doing in light of your circumstances.

"Be free to be wise. Be free to see. Be free to live. Be free to love.

"Be free to be in joy and peace.

"Know that the wise stage manager sees the vast unfolding possibilities; sees past, present, and future as one. You can know this mind, as you are a part of this consciousness. The future is not set in stone. It can be changed. It is just a system of probabilities, but in the vast possibilities, even this system is easily upended.

"You must know from the very depths of you that this is True, that this is Reality, that this is where you, your Truest Self is.

"Believe the impossible.
Live the Dream Reality.
Know that all unfolds for the highest and best.
Trust the inner wisdom of the manifested Light.
Call forth the Truth of what is always possible in any given situation.

"This is where you can live. This is where you are free. This is where your Truest Self already is. Aligning yourself here is aligning yourself with your Core Reality. There is a measure of Reality in everything, but it is veiled, hidden, until you awaken. It does not mean abandoning your life. It means embracing it. It does not mean cutting yourself off, but loving all of it, and yourself in the midst of it. You live from awareness. You perceive the Divine Drama and your part in the midst of it. But in this awareness and perception you are free of it.

"Dwell here. Dwell in this vast and free space, my beloved. Do not buy into the drama. Just live in the midst of the drama, totally free, totally in joy, totally in love, totally in peace. This is wisdom of the deepest order. You are loved and beloved. This is your birthright. You are loved infinitely and held in infinite light. You are always here. The transient circumstances do not negate anything of this Truest Reality. They can only enhance it.

"Dwell here with me, my beloved one. Dwell where no doubt, no fear, no conflict, and no harm can disturb. Dwell here where all of the treasures of my realm are yours forever. Dwell here where everything is well and where all is love. Dwell here where we are One, where we are never apart. Dwell here with me in infinite, beautiful oneness of everlasting joy and bliss.

"There is great power for healing here. This is where the stars in their courses were laid. This is where the design of the entire universes is held. You are here. Your Truest Self is always here. If you can remain here in your consciousness, your bliss will transfigure you into a star of bright light. You already are this bright light, but living here in consciousness will bring it forth for all to see and for you to enjoy. There is so much joy here. It expands everywhere into everyone and everything if you live here in consciousness. Dwell in this infinite vast place. This is your Truest Reality. So be it.

"Blessed be the One who dwells in infinite Light. Blessed is the One who is Love. Blessed are all the manifest forms of the Exalted One. Blessed are you. When you live in this state of blessedness it is as though miracles trail behind you. You may not even be aware, but they do. Miracles follow you. The Light you are, if you live in this Light, can bring healings, transformations and awakenings that people cannot dream of now. Yet, they are possible, even probable and expected, if you live in Light. Can you live here in this wisdom? Yes you can."

I heard the Divine say,

"You are blessed. All are blessed. Dwell in the wisdom of infinite possibilities. Dwell with Me here, my beloved."

WORKBOOK
Questions

• Describe a wise person.

• How are you wise and when have you been wise?

• How can you dwell in both the wisdom of knowing what you know to be true and also the humility and adventure of mystery?

- Why is love necessary for true wisdom?

- What limiting beliefs are you ready to let go of?

- If there were no limits to the possibilities of your dreams, what would you do?

Meditations

Mandala Meditation

Mandalas are intuitive representations of All That Is. They are found in every culture and spirituality: Native American medicine wheels, Celtic labyrinths, and Tibetan sand mandalas are just a few examples.

Circles provide the basis for a mandala, with a center and then layers depicting levels of manifested reality. Some of the designs in mandalas are geometric, while others use the flora and fauna of Nature. Generally, though, they are symbolic and use a wide variety of colors.

To use a mandala for meditation you can find a picture of one that grabs your attention online or in a book, or you can make your own after looking at a few and getting the general idea. Then follow these steps:

1) First, open yourself to your highest and best good only. Ask for guidance for what is appropriate for what you need right now.

2) Then focus your energy through the third eye area (the lower center of your forehead between your eyebrows) and look intently at the whole mandala. Just take it all in without focusing on any one thing. Notice any impressions, feelings, or thoughts that arise. Notice them and then let them go.

3) When you are ready, shift your concentration to the center of the mandala. What arises within you now? What is the center teaching you?

4) Now move to the next layer right around the center. What do you see? What is the significance of this?

5) Continue repeating step #4 with each layer until you reach the outer layer, asking these same questions at each level and any other questions that may arise.

6) Again dwell on the whole, taking it all in. What arises in you now?

7) When you are done, write down any reflections, insights, and guidance you received for your life. You may also want to lie down, breathe slowly and purposefully, and place the picture of the mandala over your third eye or any other place on your body where you feel intuitively to do so. Ask that you receive the wisdom and energy of the mandala, of course, for your highest and best.

Write down any new questions, insights, or experiences here.

Fast-Forward Meditation

For this meditation, you will be fast-forwarding into the future to find a place of unlimited possibilities.

First, find a quiet, undisturbed place to lie down comfortably. Begin a form of pranayama (breathwork) yoga by breathing in twice through the mouth followed by breathing out through the mouth. This double breathwork is described in detail at the end of chapter two. Take two intake breaths then one outbreath. Breathe this way gently and rhythmically for a few minutes but no longer than ten minutes.

When your body is relaxed, set your intention to go to a time in your future when you are totally safe and totally well and when you are living in the infinite possibilities available to you. Don't think about this; just go there in your awareness. Just go to this positive, unlimited future. Then answer these questions:

- What year are you in? Do you know the month or day?

- What visual images, sensations, smells, sounds, tastes are you picking up?

- What is happening? What work are you doing? Who are you with? Where are you living? How is your body?

- What are you thinking about? What are you feeling emotionally? Just spend time enjoying these feelings and experiences.

- What are you supposed to learn from this meditation? What are you supposed to take back with you from the future to your present time?

- What do you now understand about the unlimited possibilities available to you?

- Write down any new questions, insights, or experiences here.

Affirmations
Chakra: Forehead/Third Eye
Color: Indigo

Variations on a Theme: "I am Wisdom."

"I dwell in the infinite possibilities."

"I perceive the highest and best for myself and all."

"All that I see is filled and surrounded with light and love."

"I release all the limiting beliefs that no longer serve my highest and best."

"I am open to my vast potential."

"I am open to knowing and unknowing."

"I marvel in mystery and magic."

Write down any new questions, insights, or experiences here.

Further Reading and Study

Orloff, Judith, MD. *Positive Energy*. NY: Harmony Books, 2004.
  —*Second Sight*. NY: Warner Books, 1996.

Choquette, Sonia. *Trust Your Vibes*. Carlsbad, CA: Hay House, 2004.

Schulz, Mona Lisa. *Awakening Intuition*. NY: Harmony Books, 1998.

Goldberg, Philip. *The Intuitive Edge*. LA: J.P. Tarcher, 1983.

Myss, Caroline. *Sacred Contracts*. NY: Harmony Books, 2001.

Dyer, Wayne. *Excuses Begone!* Carlsbad, CA: Hay House, 2009.

Peale, Norman Vincent. *The Power of Positive Thinking*. NY: Fawcett Columbine, 1956.

8

You are Whole

I heard the Divine say, "Tell the people:

"You are whole. You are always in well-beingness. This is your Truest Nature.

"Wholeness is a state of being that is always true. At your core level you are always whole. Nothing is amiss. Nothing is lacking. All is possible.

"You are the breath of Spirit, the idea of God. In its original state perfect and pure. You are a ray of God that has shone down into material existence. In this existence you experience brokenness and struggle, but this is so that you can learn all the facets of material existence.

"You are God becoming God again, re-growing through awareness back into your original wholeness and oneness. Yet, your Truest Self has never left, is ever one and whole.

"You are like a ray of sunlight that shines down to the earth. Your existence here is like a solar-powered lighthouse full of mirrors and windows. The ray from the sun gives light to power your existence and the mirrors reflect the sun's ray during the day and the solar-powered cells shine your light at night. Your light is so bright. In the day-to-day existence you accumulate the dust and the dirt. It is important to clean your internal mirrors, that is, your subconscious, to keep your energy strong. Clean your windows, your thoughts, and emotions so you shine the pure light of the sunray you are as best you can on this earth.

"You find your way to wholeness through brokenness and then you find you can keep growing in wholeness not through brokenness, but through joy and releasing whatever is not true to the sunray.

"You do not need to identify anymore with the brokenness or impurity that clings. You are not the dirt on the windows or mirrors of the lighthouse. You are the sun, shining a ray into material existence. Just release the dirt, release it and be done with it. Do not think you are the dirt. Release the past. Release the brokenness. Release. Release. Release. You are whole. You are always well, my beloved. You are always. You are.

"When you operate from your emotional wholeness you operate from your Truest Self. Emotional wellness means you are open to all of the emotions that pass through you. It may or may not mean actually emoting. Many times it is enough to notice or acknowledge and honor the emotions that may arise without actually feeling them.

"This is not denial of emotions. It is better to feel them than not. When you have learned to be open to all your feelings and you can process them without denying or repressing them, then you can graduate to the next level, which is allowing your feelings to flow through you without necessarily emoting them.

"You can say to them, 'I see you grief. Thank you for arising in me and helping me to learn another place that I can let go of attachment to what is temporary and fleeting. I honor you. I allow you to pass through me without attaching to who I am.' Then the energy of the emotion can pass right through you.

"It is okay if you are unable to shift from the flow of emoting into the flow of allowing emotional energy to pass through you. Sometimes both may happen. It is easier on your body to allow emotional energy to pass through, but if one cannot let the emotions just pass through, then it is okay to emote them, and, in fact, it is better for the body to feel them in this case.

"Try not to judge your emotions by calling them 'bad.' By attaching a judgment to them, you energize the emotions and create attachments to them. The more you can neutralize your perception of emotions, just accepting them without judging them, the easier it is to allow them to pass through without emoting them. The more you judge emotions as bad, the more attachments you will have to them and it will be more difficult to stay centered in your Truest Self.

"Your emotional well-being is derived from your mental well-being. When your beliefs and thoughts are healthy and expansive your emotional well-being is strong, too. Likewise, when you have limiting beliefs and unloving thoughts your emotional energy is going to dwell in this state of heaviness.

Your physical well-being is also derivative of your mental and emotional well-being, although other factors play a part. Your body is more likely to thrive when your mental and emotional states are healthy.

"But really all is one. A sick body can produce a downturn of emotions and thoughts. A healthy body can make emotions and thoughts lighter. And all is derived from your spiritual health. A strong spirit can make even a sickly body last for many, many years. A weak soul can turn an otherwise healthy body into one of disease.

"The awareness of wholeness is a giant step forward in your consciousness. When you allow yourself, spirit, mind, emotions, and body to live from this awareness, you create more wholeness in you and around you. Wholeness begets wholeness. All eventually begets wholeness. Even sickness and destruction eventually lead to more wholeness. But why take that path? Take the path that leads directly to more wholeness.

"Wholeness is your natural state. It is not unnatural. However, in your state of awareness you see only part of the wholeness, so you are growing into wholeness. Yet within you is the wholeness you seek. You are what you seek. Yes. You must embrace all in order that all may be transformed—all the joy and all the suffering.

"It does not mean you need to take on all the suffering, just be open to all the suffering so that all may heal. Anything you put aside will fragment and need to be reintegrated later.

"Embrace all people and you will embrace the whole that is within you. It does not mean tolerating all—that anything goes.

"It means knowing that deep within all is love—the light of all that is only love. The predator mistakenly destroys to save. The prey mistakenly flees to save. But this is the duality of existence. Both are rooted in love. Both are driven by fear. When fear is removed and the love that is always there is revealed, the dualistic chase disappears and all that is left is wholeness and love. You are pure love, whole love. That is who you are. Everything else is but a passing dream. You are whole. You are well. You are always well. All is very well.

"Wholeness comes when you are able to embrace both poles of a duality and then transcend them.

"At the time of your life when it seems the darkest, this is the moment you may uncover your Truest Light.

"At times of your life, when you feel worthless, hopeless, unloved, and powerless, these are liminal times. When you think that all is lost, all is not lost. All is never lost. But feeling that all is lost, the cry of utter despair, the pain of abject suffering causes you to touch a very deep place within your being. A place that is holy. A place where I Am.

"The corest of pains drives you even deeper, to find a place within that no hate can ever touch, no suffering can ever harm, and no injustice will ever mar. When you feel all is lost, allow yourself to be with this deep pain. Do not be afraid of the deep pain. Allow it to be. When you can hold this space and not resist, you will be at a divine threshold.

"You will find strength in your time of feeling powerlessness. You will find infinite self-value in your time of feeling worthless. You will find an unbounded love when you think you are totally unlovable. You will discover the hope that undergirds all and has turned lives, families, and even nations around.

"Be in this place with yourself. Be within. Be.

"Whatever you have experienced that has left you feeling worthless, unloved, hopeless, or powerless is bringing you to the point where you can embrace who you really are. Your painful feelings do not have to drive you to the point of despair. No, they can drive you to the point where your suffering reveals to you that you don't need to feel any of these things, because they are not really true to who you are.

"Your feelings of worthlessness that feel so terrible can bring you to your Truest Self. There, you realize your feelings are letting you know something very important. It is time for change. It is time to be who you Really are. Your beliefs that you are worthless, unloved, powerless, or without hope are too small for you now. It is time to grow into the larger beliefs of your Truest Self.

"Know, too, that whatever has driven you to believe these things about yourself and therefore to have such painful feelings, is trying to help you. Yes, everything that is painful ultimately is trying to help you, to heal you, to show you that you are love, you are light, you are whole. You are.

"To live in wholeness it is important to live in the present moment. At this very moment, what do you need? Most likely in this very moment, you are fine. In the next moment, you may notice your body needs hydration and so you get up and respond to your body's requirements. But you, your Truest Self is continually in wholeness.

"This is how you can live your entire life, my beloved one. Moment to moment in the now.

"The past no longer exists but in your memory, so no need to live there. The future does not yet exist so worrying about something that does not exist is just a drain on your energy and your life force. When you live moment to moment in the now, your needs disappear, you live in the flow of Spirit.

"This flow of Spirit is not mediated by any one or any thing. It simply is. It is who you are and is an expression of everything around you.

"This flow of Spirit causes you only to be aware. In the moment you know how to allow thoughts, feelings, words, and actions to arise and to depart without attaching. You become the Flow that you are at the level of your Truest Self. You know what you are to say or not say, to do or not do. Future decisions are left for the future. The past is remembered and stored, even embraced and cherished. All is consumed in love.

"Each person is responsible for his or her own words and actions, even the energy of their thoughts and feelings. Yet, you can live from your Truest Self, where your identity is not attached to them.

"Your Truest Self is always in the moment. This is how you can live out your wholeness of everything that you are. No need to dwell anywhere else, because there is not anywhere else except as an imagination in the mind. All is now. Wholeness is now. You are now, my beloved one. Be in the now. Be.

"When you are one with the Flow, you do not need to rush it, push it, or block it. The Flow, when you are one with it, goes at its own pace and speed. Sometimes more rapidly, sometimes more slowly, but when you are One you are operating moment by moment with it.

"In this sense then, you are not 'making things happen' as is commonly understood in your cultural mindset. When you are one with the Flow 'you' as separate ego self do not exist. Your Truest Self is always present and always one with the Flow, so when you live from your Truest Self, trying to control your destiny really doesn't make sense anymore.

"Rather in your Truest Self, in your wholeness, you are moment by moment already living your destiny, already creating your Truest Life.

"There is a subtle distinction here. It is not about making rigid plans; it is about consciously living the Plan that is unfolding. Whether you are aware of it or not, whether you are living in full conscious participation or not, doesn't matter. It still flows and unfolds. All of your hindrances are trying to get you to live in this unfolding that continually reveals your wholeness that is. You are blocked to help you dive deeper than the level at which you are living. See your blocks as reminders that you are now swimming at a depth too shallow for your spiritual skill. Go deeper; the blocks aren't there anymore.

"Flow flows well with One Mind. Double-mindedness can be a hindrance to the mysterious Flow of All.

"Your wholeness is ever-present, waiting to be tapped into, so it can be revealed in and through you. When you live in wholeness, there is great ease to your life. It is just One Flow like a twig floating on a mighty river, with no concern as to its destiny, just riding the waves of being. Then you will pass over into the vast Beingness of all, like the river merging at last with the ocean. Your consciousness is returning home. Your Truest Self is already home.

"The task before you is to heal yourself. Heal into the oneness, into the wholeness that you are. Keep integrating, keep exposing within yourself whatever is not your Truest Self and then release it. Release what is not true to You to reveal what is true to You. Release whatever is not love, light, joy, wisdom, peace, security, truth, wholeness, etc. Just let it go. It is not really you—it is just attached to you.

"You might think this is who you are. You might think these other things are part of your identity, but they are not. They are just temporary attachments, to help you learn lessons. That is all. When you have learned the lessons of Light, you do not need these attachments, so just let them go. Just be.

"You are always held in wholeness, whether you know it or not, whether you participate consciously with it or not. I am always holding all in loving awareness. Join me in this healing of wholeness.

"There is no single path to healing and wholeness. All create and take their own path. Can you dwell in the wholeness that is everlasting and evermore? You can. Your divine spark, your Truest Self, is already there, already here. It can take time to raise your consciousness to this level and remain in this energy for long periods of time. In Reality, there is no time, you are already there, but as you work these things out at the various levels of divine manifestation, you can use time to help you regain longer awareness of the Divine in you.

"Your wholeness is ever-present and ever-dwelling in the bright array of manifested light. Your being dwells here at all times. Your wholeness is centered here. It never leaves. But as you have descended into the levels of time immemorial you have forgotten the True State of being you are. As you remember, you rise. As you integrate, you rise further. As you love, you embrace your entire Truest Self.

"Of course, your Truest Self in wholeness is infinite so you can ever-expand into this eternal wholeness. Your body is just a vehicle to help you at this stage of your spiritual evolution back into your eternal home. At some point in your incarnations, you no longer will need a body to learn what you want to learn.

"You are a bright light shining in the firmament. Your presence alone is beginning to heal others. Do not be afraid to look into the depths of another. Doing so can heal them in an instant at the soul level. Look and open your heart and they will heal. You are doing so well, my beloved.

"Dwell with me evermore in my eternal wholeness. Dwell with me. Be with me.

"Be Secure.
Be Content.
Be Joy.
Be Love.
Be Truth.
Be Wise.
Be Light.
Be Whole.
Be.

"Your Truest Self is already all of these things and more. Your Truest Self and I are one in the infinite dance of love and play.

"Be well. All is well. Blessed be the Wholeness that holds all in an eternal embrace of compassionate Love and Light. Blessed be All who were birthed in this glorious Light.

"From Light and Wholeness you came. From there all shall return till the Light that fills the universe is revealed—full and true in joyous communion. In this awareness you are. In this awareness you are held. In this awareness you are revealed.

"All is well. All is whole. All is continuously created and consummated in the passionate fire of beingness and non-beingness.

"Blessed are you. You bring the Light of my Being to All.

"Blessed, you are. The Light of All shines in you, through you, and comes from others mirrored back to you."

I heard the Divine say,

"You are my beloved always and forever more. You are whole. You are Love.

"Blessed be."

WORKBOOK
Questions

- What does wholeness mean to you?

- How do you interpret wholeness in light of disease, disability, and death?

- Describe how wholeness is a state of mind, quality of being, something to strive for in order to achieve, all of these, or something altogether different.

- How are healing and wholeness connected?

- If your Truest Self is always well and whole, how can you tap into this reality in order to live your life?

Meditations

Sacred Word Meditation

Another name for sacred word meditation is Centering Prayer. In this meditation, you simply rest in the Divine Indwelling. Rather than trying to do anything at all, like empty your mind of thoughts, you just rest in Sacred Presence.

You may notice you have thoughts, feelings, and sensory perceptions come up, but rather than getting rid of them, you just gently return to a sacred word you have chosen and then rest again in wholeness without attaching to anything. If you notice you are attaching to a thought or image, just again return to the sacred word and the quieting of your soul. I like to use the sacred word, "Beloved," but you can choose any sacred word that is meaningful to you: Love, Joy, Christ, Mary, Buddha, Shiva, God, etc. It is best to stay with the same sacred word over time.

For beginners, build success by taking small steps. Perhaps five minutes in the morning before the kids get up or five minutes during your lunch hour is all you can manage at first. That's great! Build slowly from there. The more you experience success the more you will want to do. In fact, if you skip your sacred word meditation for a day or two after being consistent for a while, you will notice you want to get back to it. You will also wonder how you got along without it!

Sacred word meditation is a great way to learn to "Be still and know that I am God" and to help your heart, mind, and soul dwell on wholeness above all else.

Write down any new questions, insights, or experiences here.

Gold Light Meditation

No matter where you are today, or what you are doing, practice this simple mantra: Say, "I am Whole" over and over again. You can say it out loud or silently, though if you can say it out loud it adds more of your senses to the meditation and increases the vitality of it. The most important thing is to repeat it with feeling, not like a robot.

As you say this mantra, you can also visualize golden, healing light entering your body through the top of your head. Watch this golden light fill every part of your body until everything is glowing and shining. Imagine that all of your cells, organs, tissues, bones, and skin are sparkling like gold diamonds. Continue to visualize this golden light as it increases in brightness to the point that it is so bright it is difficult to look at—like looking directly into the sun with the naked eye. Then imagine this golden light extending beyond your body a few feet until you are enveloped in a large oval of golden wholeness. This will help your body heal and help you feel more energized.

Write down any new questions, insights, or experiences here.

Affirmations

Chakra: Overall Energy

Color: Gold

Variations on a Theme: "I am Whole."

"I am healing and growing into wholeness at the right pace for me."

"All is well. All is well with my soul."

"Health and wholeness are my truest nature."

"My wholeness is not dependent on my circumstances."
"I perceive the perfection in and through and behind all."
"I am whole and am a part of the wholeness of the Divine."
Write down any new questions, insights, or experiences here.

Further Reading and Study

Tolle, Eckhart. *The Power of Now*. Novato, CA: New World Library, 1999.

de Mello, Anthony. *Awareness*. NY: Image Books/Doubleday, 1992.

McDowell, Monica. *My Karma Ran Over My Dogma*. Seattle: Healing Light, 2007.

Eckhart, Meister. *Everything as Divine*. NY: Paulist Press, 1996.

Keating, Thomas. *Manifesting God*. NY: Lantern Books, 2006.

Panikkar, Raimon. *The Experience of God: Icons of the Mystery*. Minneapolis: Fortress Press, 2006.

Conclusion

You Are

The Great I Am is experimenting and playing in and through all forms of manifested Light. You are participating in this great experiment. The more you connect with and live from your Truest Self, the more Light and Love become full reality in the created orders.

The Beingness that is in and through all is in you and working through you, whether you are conscious of this or not. As you become more in tune with your Divine Light, your awareness grows, and the Beingness in you becomes One movement of Love, working directly through consciousness rather than indirectly out of shadow, unconsciousness, and unawareness.

The Beingness That Is loves you, believes in you, hopes in you, creates in you. This is the Reality that weaves under, in, and through all that you see and all that you are. You can never escape it for you are it. You are.

Say, "I am," and breathe deeply into your core. Say, "I am," and know that you are.

Divine Blessing

May the Light that is in you shine brightly for all to see.
May the Loving Flame of all bring warmth to your heart.
May the Divine Heart so encompass you
and flow into your own soul's journey
that everything you do is blessed
with rich and overflowing Light and Love.
So may it be and so it is.

Postscript

Why I Write: The Call

In mid-January of 2008, an unexpected visitor dropped by my house one evening—God.

It was about seven p.m., and I was relishing a rare triple treat: the house was clean, the humming dishwasher was rinsing away our dinner's crumbs, and my children were studiously finishing their homework. All was well. To make the most of it, I scurried off to my bedroom for a much needed mommy rest. Stretching out on my bed, I sunk my body into the comforting depths of the downy covers, and started breathing rhythmically and mindfully—one of my favorite ways to practice some good old-fashioned self-care.

When all of a sudden, hot molten energy started running from the top of my head to the bottom of my tailbone, over and over again, completely obliterating the myth that lightning never strikes in the same place twice.

Uh-oh. Now what? I said to myself.

Mystical experiences were hardly a new thing for me. I had begun having them in dump truck loads during my years as a whistle-blowing clergywoman. (See my book, *My Karma Ran Over My Dogma*, for the particulars on that humdinger of a saga.) But this experience was especially unique, not just because of the intensity of the energy surging down my spine, but also because of what occurred next.

While I lay there, I kept my eyes closed in fierce concentration, willing myself not to spontaneously combust in a fiery cremation (as if I had any control at all over what was happening to me...ha!). After awhile—I don't know how long as time usually stands still during these experiences—I started wondering when the searing of my nervous system was finally going to end. Feeling both cautious and curious, I opened my eyes, hoping to get my bearings. I'll confess: I was disappointed to find that I was still in my room (No bilocation? Drats!), and I was still on my bed (Not even levitating? Double drats!)

Then just when I thought it was going to be among the more "ordinary" mystical experiences I'd had...well, umm, how should I put this? The only way I can think of is to just tell it like it happened:

Quite literally, above me, "a portal from heaven opened and a light shone down upon me, and the voice of the Lord spoke unto me saying, 'Will you write for me? Will you be a voice for me?'"

Gosh, it was like it had come right out of the Bible. As I mused about this epiphany later, I could just hear the skeptics' taunts: "Oh puh-leeeze. How predictable. Don't you think in the last few thousand years the Almighty could have come up with some new means of revelation? A light shining down from a portal in heaven? Bite me! At least think of something original. I bet your next experience will be a burning bush..."

Honestly, I have no explanation to give to these hypothetical skeptics. Nothing. Nada. Zip. It seems they make a pretty good point. Why didn't God come in some uncommon way? I don't know. Maybe God thinks, "if it ain't broke, don't fix it." I really have no idea. But, I'd had enough mystical experiences up to this point in my life, not to doubt what had happened that evening. To me, it was as real as the chair I am sitting in as I type these words. You, on the other hand, are welcome to any opinion you'd like about the authenticity of this divine drop-in—or the state of my mental health.

However, the few people I have told this incident to have all had a completely different take on it: "I wish God would show up and tell me what to do."

I have replied every time, "Are you sure about that? God showed up and told me what to do (or rather, gave a very strong hint as to what I was to do) and I didn't like it one bit."

The truth is, although I like to write, I do not enjoy *being a writer* day after day after day. I find it a grueling task, and believe me, I can find a gazillion other things to do to avoid it — such as cleaning out the kitty litter, clipping embarrassing nose hairs, and watching a few exciting hours on The Weather Channel. And to say that I am not a big fan of public speaking is a *huge* understatement—like saying Hurricane Katrina was balmy with a few scattered showers. In seminary I used to rival a first-rate bulimic, routinely emptying the contents of my stomach right before speech class whenever it was my turn to read a few paltry sentences out loud to my peers.

In the years since then, I have learned how to rein in the fluttering mammoths in my stomach whether I stand up to speak in front of a few dozen or several hundred. I have even begun to—wait for it—*treasure* the immediate rapport I feel emerge between orator and audience. On many occasions I have had the privilege of witnessing the significant healing energy that can be channeled through the human voice as well as the written word.

Nevertheless, I was still not happy that writing and speaking were the two main ingredients of God's recipe for my life. So I will divulge, even at the risk of looking a tad Jonah-esque, that after the Light from heaven spoke its requests to me, I did what any self-respecting mystic would do: I *argued* with it.

"But God, you know I don't like being a writer," I complained, feeling a strong affinity to all the prophets of yore who found little comfort in a divine call. "I want to do healing work."

Apparently, not in the least bit offended or deterred, the Divine gently repeated Her requests a second time, along with a promise: "I will bring you healing work. Will you write for me?

Will you be a voice for me?"

I wasn't going to give in that easy, so I continued my protest, becoming the consummate model of rational pragmatism: "But I'm not making enough money. We need more money, and writing at home all day doesn't exactly bring it in."

"I will bring you what you need," was the next promise I received, followed by the requests being made a biblical third time: "Will you write for me? Will you be a voice for me?"

Realizing the futility of fighting with fate, something I should have already learned from my several year saga, I gave a deep, surrendering sigh, and said reluctantly, "Okay."

It must have been enough of a yes, because just as quickly as the Light had appeared, it disappeared, the portal closed, and the golden lava in my spine dissolved. So, in the end the Light won. Of course.

I must also confess, however, that it really wasn't news to me that God wanted me to write. For several months prior, I had been receiving a steady stream of words flowing into my brain, coming from, I presumed, Spirit. I had dutifully typed the words as they came, not really knowing what to do with them. It would take me yet another year to figure that out.

The result is this book.

I'm wondering about you, though. Do you know what your life purpose is? Maybe you know exactly what it is, and you keep putting it off, pushing the idea out of the frontal lobes of your attention, because the thought of it is just a bit too uncomfortable to allow it to settle in the living room of your life. You might have to go back to school! You might have to marry (or divorce)! You might have to quit! You might have to move! You might have to _____ (you fill in the blank). The only remedy is to work through your reluctance, your fears, and your insecurities, and then seize the new opportunities that come your way.

Perhaps, however, you don't know your destiny. You wish you did know exactly what the Sacred One was asking of you. You feel stuck, stymied, and totally mired in self-doubt or any number of heavy feelings and thoughts that keep you from finding the light in the darkness. Take heart! You are not alone. You are working through exactly what you need to be working on right now at this moment. Trust your process. Trust the bigger picture. Your path will eventually be illuminated; the companions of joy, love, and peace might even surprise you along the way. Find humans, too, who can accompany you on your journey, be they counselors, healers, life coaches, or friends.

No matter whether you're reluctant, lost, or living out your higher purpose, ultimately every step of the way is a precious jewel in the beautiful crown that is your life. Never forget, the Beloved sees you, knows you, and loves you every moment of every day. You are forever held in arms of Light. I know. I've seen that Light. I've heard Love speak. That is why I write.

Acknowledgments

I am so grateful for all the healers and teachers in my life, including my family, friends, and clients. I have seen the Beloved in each of you. If only you knew how much beauty you hold right inside your very being. I hope, *You are Light,* assists in that regard! This book is my humble thanks offered back to you for helping me bring more light to my own awareness.

To all the staff at O-Books who made this book a reality: Thank-you, thank-you, thank-you from the bottom of my heart and soul. Namaste!

To the Beloved, who is in all and through all and holds all together in brilliantly, jewel-toned vibrations of Oneness: May this book help bring the illumination you desire, that all may joyfully awaken to their Truest Selves.

About the Author

Monica McDowell is a dynamic speaker, inspirational author, and extraordinary practitioner in the areas of energy healing and mystical spirituality. She has the distinction of being the first ordained minister in the United States granted civil rights by a federal court. Her first book, *My Karma Ran Over My Dogma: Lessons Learned by a Whistle-Blowing Minister Turned Mystic* (2007), is a narrative of her journey through these precedent-setting legal events into life-changing mysticism and a luminous spirituality.

Monica earned her Master of Divinity degree from Princeton Theological Seminary with an emphasis in spiritual care and counseling, and she is the founder of Women's Sanctuary, offering inter-spirituality gatherings for women of all faiths. She also regularly holds workshops, classes, and retreats for budding mystics and emergent healers in the Pacific Northwest of the United States. Monica lives with her husband, two teenagers, a dog (Ruffles), and a cat (Snuffles) in Seattle, Washington.

To learn more about her work, visit her website at
www.monicamcdowell.com
or contact her at monica@monicamcdowell.com

BOOKS

O is a symbol of the world, of oneness and unity. In different cultures it also means the "eye," symbolizing knowledge and insight. We aim to publish books that are accessible, constructive and that challenge accepted opinion, both that of academia and the "moral majority."

Our books are available in all good English language bookstores worldwide. If you don't see the book on the shelves ask the bookstore to order it for you, quoting the ISBN number and title. Alternatively you can order online (all major online retail sites carry our titles) or contact the distributor in the relevant country, listed on the copyright page.

See our website www.o-books.net for a full list of over 500 titles, growing by 100 a year.

And tune in to myspiritradio.com for our book review radio show, hosted by June-Elleni Laine, where you can listen to the authors discussing their books.

mySpiritRadio